Editor

Brent L. Fox, M. Ed.

Editor in Chief

Karen J. Goldfluss, M.S. Ed.

Creative Director

Sarah M. Fournier

Cover Artist

Sarah Kim

Illustrator

Kelly McMahon

Art Coordinator

Renée Mc Elwee

Imaging

Amanda R. Harter

Publisher

Mary D. Smith, M.S. Ed.

- Start the day off right with engaging reading and writing activities

- 85 high-interest fiction and non-fiction passages organized by theme

- Reading passages include standards-based questions reinforcing essential comprehension skills

- Culminating writing activity in each unit encourages students to revisit multiple reading passages

Teacher Created Resources

Author

Ruth Foster, M. Ed.

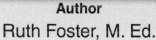

For correlations to the Common Core State Standards, visit *http://www.teachercreated.com/standards/*.

Teacher Created Resources

12621 Western Avenue
Garden Grove, CA 92841
www.teachercreated.com

ISBN: 978-1-4206-8123-9

© *2018 Teacher Created Resources*
Made in U.S.A.

Table of Contents

Table of Contents (cont.)

Introduction

Reading should be something that students look forward to. However, sometimes students must find fun and accessible literature *before* they can realize how enjoyable reading can be! The passages in this book contain high-interest topics that will immediately hook even the most stubborn of readers. Fun themes, surprise twists, and grade-appropriate content will motivate and excite young readers. Additionally, the passages in this book were designed to be accessible to students of varying reading abilities. Basic sight words are introduced and then reinforced with repetition and practice. As new words are introduced, they are repeated and written into the story in ways that allow a student to use context clues to decipher their meanings.

Each unit begins with five reading passages. The first several passages are short and include three multiple-choice questions. The remaining passages are a bit longer and have four multiple-choice questions. The passages in each unit are a mixture of fact and fiction. The last page of the unit calls for a written response to a prompt that incorporates the theme of the unit.

The passages in each unit are all linked by a loose theme. As the students continue to read more of the unit, they will begin to discover the common thread that weaves together each collection of stories. This approach broadens a student's comprehension and understanding of the subject matter. It allows students to practice new words in various stories and in different genres. It also shows students how separate passages can be linked with other passages and used collectively to expand one's horizons and views. This approach ultimately allows students to become familiar with the flexibility of word use, different viewpoints, and how we can learn from both fiction and nonfiction texts.

All of the texts and activities in the *Let's Get This Day Started* series have been aligned to the Common Core State Standards (CCSS). Visit *http://www.teachercreated.com/ standards/* for all standards correlations.

Using the Book

Teachers should not feel restricted by a daily warm-up activity. Sometimes, schedules change. A morning assembly, a make-up lesson, or just an extra-busy day can easily throw off the classroom schedule for days. A teacher never knows what his or her week is going to look like. *Let's Get This Day Started* does not need to be completed every day or even every other day. Teachers can take their time and arrange the activities to fit their own schedules. The book is written so the teacher can stop wherever and whenever he or she wants. A teacher may choose to do a unit a week (one passage a day), or at other times, spread a unit out over a few weeks. There is no right or wrong way.

At the beginning of the year, a teacher may choose to have the class read the passages together as a group before asking them to read each passage again on their own. A teacher may also choose to have students reread passages several weeks later to practice fluidity or so that the students can see how "easy" the passages have become.

The multiple-choice questions in *Let's Get This Day Started* assess all levels of comprehension—from recall to critical thinking. The questions are based on fundamental reading skills found in scope-and-sequence charts across the nation. Examples of just some of the question styles used in this series include:

- recalling information
- sequencing in chronological order
- using prior knowledge
- identifying synonyms and antonyms
- visualizing
- knowing and using grade-level vocabulary

- recognizing the main idea
- using context clues to understand new words
- identifying supporting details
- making inferences
- understanding cause and effect
- drawing conclusions

All question stems and answers are written so that they are a continuation of reading practice and critical thinking. If an answer choice includes an unfamiliar word, the correct answer can still be found by the process of elimination. Remind students to read every answer choice! If the answer doesn't jump out at them, they can get it right by crossing out the wrong answers first.

The written response (Write On!) pages require students to look back at the passages they have read in each unit for facts, ideas, or vocabulary. Students are encouraged to respond creatively to a variety of fun writing prompts and then support their answers by referring back to examples from several of the reading passages.

Use the Tracking Sheet on page 108 to keep track of which passages you have given to your students, or distribute copies of the sheet for students to monitor their own progress.

Name: _____

A Slow Animal

You sleep in a bed. Think about how long your bed is. How long would it take you to walk from one end of your bed to the other? It would not take long. You could do it in seconds! You could do it fast, fast, fast!

Some animals cannot go fast. One animal is the sloth. The sloth is a very slow animal. You can go a lot faster than a sloth. You could do it in a few seconds, but it would take a sloth a *minute*. A minute is *60* seconds. The sloth is slow, slow, slow.

Sloths do not sleep in beds. They sleep in trees. They hang upside down while they sleep. They move and eat while hanging upside down, too.

1. This story is mainly about
   a. seconds.
   b. hanging upside down.
   c. a slow animal.
   d. how long your bed is.

2. A minute is
   a. 6 seconds.
   b. 60 seconds.
   c. 66 seconds.
   d. 600 seconds.

3. If you saw a sloth, it would most likely be
   a. hanging upside down.
   b. sleeping.
   c. eating.
   d. moving fast.

Name: _____

What Animal Am I?

Noah went first. He said, "I have a mane. I have a tail. I am a big cat." Then, he roared. All the children knew what Noah was once he roared. They knew that Noah was a lion because lions are cats that have manes and tails. Lions are cats that roar.

It was Violet's turn. Violet stood up. She started to walk to the front of the class. She did not walk fast. She walked slowly. She walked so slowly that the children got mad. "Move faster, Violet!" they said. "Hurry up! We want to know what animal you are."

Violet did not move faster. She did not move faster because she was a sloth!

1. Why did the children get mad?

   a. Violet did not seem to take her turn.

   b. Violet walked too fast.

   c. They wanted Violet to roar.

   d. They did not know Violet was a sloth.

2. If Violet had hopped to the front of the class, she would most likely be a

   a. snake.   b. fish.   c. dog.   d. bunny.

3. What title fits this story best?

   a. "The Mad Children"

   b. "Violet's Animal"

   c. "The Front of the Class"

   d. "All About Sloths"

Name: _____

When a Sloth Is Cold

A Poem About Sloths

I am told
That when a sloth is cold
It cannot shiver.

A sloth can't shiver?
How can that be?
Are you teasing me?

Muscles, muscles, that's what we use
When we shiver and shake to warm up and move.
Muscles, muscles, a sloth just doesn't have enough.
It can't shiver or shake or do any of that stuff.

It seems funny
That a sloth must stay where it is warm and sunny.
You and I can play in snow and ice
And find it all to be very nice.

1. Why can't a sloth shiver?

   a. It lives where it is warm and sunny.

   b. It doesn't get cold.

   c. It doesn't have enough muscles.

   d. It plays all day.

2. "When a Sloth Is Cold" is a

   a. poem.   b. song.   c. story.   d. sentence.

3. Look at the last words of each line. Some of the words rhyme. Which answer does **not** use rhyming words?

   a. sunny, funny

   b. enough, stuff

   c. told, cold

   d. muscles, move

Name: _____

Green Hair

Look in the trees. You see green leaves. A sloth may be hanging upside down in the tree, but you may not see it! The sloth is hard to see because it stays very still. It does not move. It is hard, sometimes, to see things when they do not move.

One more thing makes the sloth hard to see. The sloth is hard to see because it looks green! The green color helps the sloth hide in the leaves. It is hard, sometimes, to see things when they are all the same color.

A sloth does not have green fur. No animal has green fur. So why does the sloth look green? The fur looks green because something grows on it. The green thing growing on the sloth's fur is algae. You may have seen algae growing in ponds or the ocean. The algae growing on the sloth is good for the sloth. It helps the sloth stay hidden. The algae is also good for something else. When the sloth is hungry, it can lick its hair! It can eat the algae!

1. A fact is something that is true. Which sentence is a fact?

    a. Sloths are green.

    b. Sloths can look green.

    c. Sloths do not eat algae.

    d. Sloths cannot stay still.

2. This story was written so that you could learn

    a. why it is hard to see a sloth.

    b. all about animal fur.

    c. why we have hair.

    d. all about what animals eat.

3. How does staying still help the sloth?

    a. It makes the sloth green.

    b. It makes the algae grow.

    c. It makes the sloth hard to see.

    d. It makes the leaves turn green.

Name: _____

The Oddest Thing

"Mama, Mama! Wake up!" Sammy said. "I saw the oddest thing. It was very strange."

"What did you see?" asked Sammy's mother as she slowly chewed on something green and tasty.

"It was on the ground. It didn't crawl! It ran! And it didn't use its hands to move! It only ran on two legs! It ran to the river and jumped in. Then, it swam away."

"That is very odd," Sammy's mother agreed. "It must not be very smart. Why didn't it crawl out on a branch and then drop into the river? That would have been safer. Was it a good swimmer?"

"It could swim as well as me," Sammy said, "but I think it was sick. It only had hair on top of its head, and the hair wasn't green. It would be hard to hide in a tree if this animal had fur that color."

"That sounds terrible," Sammy's mother said. "I am sorry you saw such a thing, but you are a smart sloth, so you know what you saw cannot be real. It is too strange. You must have been dreaming."

1. When something is *odd*, it is

   a. tasty.   **b.** smart.   **c.** dreaming.   **d.** strange.

2. Why did the author wait until the end before telling you Sammy was a sloth?

   a. to surprise you

   b. to make you think that you were dreaming

   c. to make you mad

   d. to show you that sloths can talk

3. Most likely, what did Sammy's mother chew on?

   a. gum   **b.** grass   **c.** leaves   **d.** fish

4. Sammy could **not** have seen

   a. a boy with blond hair.   **c.** a girl with red hair.

   b. a dog with brown fur.   **d.** a man with black hair.

Name: _____

Write On!

A **Name Poem** tells about the word. It uses the letters of the word for the first letter of each line. A Name Poem is also called an *Acrostic Poem*.

For example, a name poem with the title "Snake" would go like this:

Snake

by Sammy Sloth

Slithers through the grass

Naps in the sun

A terrible thing if it is in your desk!

Kind of reptile

Eats mice and frogs

Look back at the stories you read about sloths. Think about what you learned from the stories. Use what you learned to write a Name Poem about a sloth.

S _____

_____

L _____

_____

O _____

_____

T _____

_____

H _____

_____

Name: _____

The Coldest

One place is the coldest. One place is the windiest. One place is the driest. What is this place? It is Antarctica. Antarctica is the coldest. It is the windiest. It is the driest. Antarctica has lots of ice. The ice is very thick. In some places, it is a mile deep! It is so cold that the ice does not melt.

The ice is not smooth. It has cracks. It moves. The moving ice is called a *glacier*. Some ice breaks off the land and falls into the ocean. The broken-off ice floats. The floating ice is called an *iceberg*. One iceberg was very big. It was as tall as a building that has 50 floors!

1. Ice that moves on land is called
   - **a.** an iceberg.
   - **b.** a building.
   - **c.** an ocean.
   - **d.** a glacier.

2. One iceberg was as
   - **a.** wide as a building with 5 floors.
   - **b.** tall as a building with 5 floors.
   - **c.** wide as a building with 50 floors.
   - **d.** tall as a building with 50 floors.

3. Antarctica is **not** the
   - **a.** coldest.
   - **b.** wettest.
   - **c.** driest.
   - **d.** windiest.

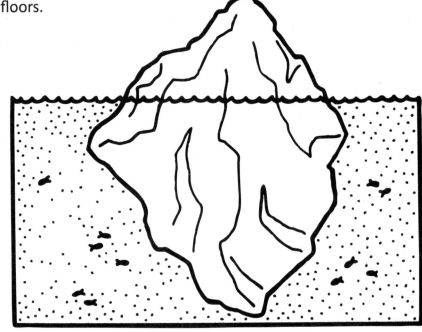

#8123 Let's Get This Day Started: Reading ©*Teacher Created Resources*

Name: _____

Danger on the Ice!

The people said, "Let's stop here. Let's eat lunch." The people started to eat. They looked out over the ice. They looked at the sea. "We like Antarctica," the people said. "It is cold, but it is beautiful."

Crack! Boom! What was that noise? The people looked at each other. They were scared. They did not know what made the crack. They did not know what made the boom. Then, the people felt funny. What was wrong with the land? The land was moving!

The people were not on land! They had stopped to eat on thick ice. The ice had broken off! Now they were floating on an iceberg! A ship had to come to save the people.

1. Why did the people feel funny?

   a. The land seemed to be moving.

   b. They had stopped to eat.

   c. They liked Antarctica.

   d. They floated on a ship.

2. Most likely, the people were wearing

   a. coats and boots.

   b. shorts and T-shirts.

   c. bathing suits and sun hats.

   d. slippers and raincoats.

3. Why did a ship have to come to save the people?

   a. The iceberg was thick.

   b. The iceberg was cold.

   c. The iceberg was part of the land.

   d. The iceberg was floating.

Name: _____

A Penguin Play

Setting: a street
Characters: a boy and a girl

The boy and girl are talking as they walk to school.

Girl: I went to the North Pole. I saw penguins and polar bears.

Boy: You are making up a story.

Girl: No, I am not. I am not making up a story.

Boy: I know you are making up a story. Polar bears live in the north, but penguins do not. Penguins live in the south. They live where the South Pole is. They live in Antarctica.

Girl: You are right. I made up a story. I made up a riddle, too. What do penguins eat for lunch?

Boy: I don't know. What?

Girl: Iceberg-ers!

Boy: Ha! Ha! Like hamburgers! I get it! Very funny!

1. From the story, you can tell that Antarctica

   a. is in the east.　　　　　　**c.** is in the north.

   b. is in the west.　　　　　　**d.** is in the south.

2. Why did the boy think the girl was making up a story?

   a. He knew that polar bears live in the south.

   b. He knew that penguins live in Antarctica.

   c. He knew that polar bears live in Antarctica.

   d. He knew that penguins live at the North Pole.

3. What might be the best answer to this riddle: *Who is a penguin's favorite aunt?*

   a. Aunt Arctica　　　　　　**c.** Aunt Riddle

   b. Aunt North Pole　　　　　**d.** Aunt America

Name: _____

A Fight

Lynne Cox was fighting. Who was she fighting? She was fighting herself! What was the fight about? The fight was about her breathing.

Lynne's body wanted her to take short breaths. Why did Lynne's body want her to take short breaths? If Lynne took short breaths, the cold, icy air she was breathing could be warmed in her mouth. Then, when the air went to her lungs, it would be warmed up.

Lynne needed to take deep breaths. She had to draw the cold, icy air deep into her lungs. Lynne forced herself to breathe deeply. She forced herself to breathe slowly. She breathed the cold, icy air deep into her lungs. It was very hard.

Why was the air so cold? Lynne was swimming to Antarctica. She had nothing to keep her warm. She was wearing only a bathing suit. Lynne swam between icebergs. She swam with penguins. She breathed in the freezing air. She was the first person to swim a mile to Antarctica!

1. Where did the air go when Lynne breathed it in?

   a. to Antarctica

   b. to her lungs

   c. to the cold, icy water

   d. to her bathing suit

2. Most likely, what word can be used to tell someone about Lynne?

   a. brave   b. sad   c. scared   d. bad

3. This story can be summed up as a story about

   a. a woman who had to make herself breathe.

   b. a woman who liked to swim with penguins.

   c. a woman who swam a mile to Antarctica.

   d. a woman who liked swimming in cold water.

4. What happened after the fight?

   a. Lynne breathed deeply.

   b. Lynne took short breaths.

   c. Lynne stopped breathing.

   d. Lynne warmed the air in her mouth.

Name: _____

Pete's Wish

Pete said, "I do not want to be black and white. I am tired of being black and white. I want to be a new color. I want to be the color of the sun when it sets. I want to be bright red!"

Pete got his wish. Pete was no longer black and white. He was bright red. Pete was happy. He did not look like any of the other penguins.

Pete dove into the water. Danger! Danger! A shark began to chase Pete. Pete had to jump onto the ice to get away. Then Pete said, "I want my back to be black again. I want my front to be white again. If a shark is looking up at me, the white helps to hide me. If a shark is looking down on me, the black also helps to hide me. I am safer if I can hide."

1. How do you know this story is fiction and not true?

   a. Penguins are not black and white.

   b. Penguins cannot swim and dive.

   c. Penguins cannot talk.

   d. Sharks do not eat penguins.

2. If Pete could get his wish at the end of the story, what colors would he be?

   a. green and orange

   b. red and yellow

   c. black and white

   d. red and orange

3. How did Pete get away from the shark?

   a. He got a new color.

   b. He jumped onto the ice.

   c. He hid.

   d. He swam to the sun.

4. Color in the penguin and show what colors the penguin should be. Think! What side will be black? What side will be white? Read the story again to help you decide.

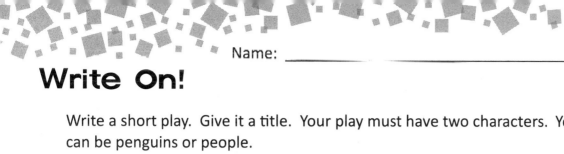

Name: _____

Write On!

Write a short play. Give it a title. Your play must have two characters. Your characters can be penguins or people.

Tell where your characters are (setting) and what they are doing.

Your characters can say or do anything you like, but you must tell your reader something about Antarctica. Think about what you learned from all the stories in this unit. Include some of that information in your play.

Title: _____

Characters: _____

Setting: _____

_____

_____

_____

_____

_____

_____

_____

_____

_____

_____

_____

Name: _____

Six Times

If you jump up, you come back down. What pulls you down? Gravity pulls you down. Earth's gravity keeps you from floating off into space.

You are on the moon. You jump up. You go up, up, up. You jump six times higher! You jump six times higher because the moon is smaller than Earth. There is less gravity pulling you down.

What if you played basketball on the moon? You would have to put the basketball hoops up very high. The ball would bounce high! When you threw the ball, the ball would go six times higher!

1. A better title for this story might be

   a. "Playing Basketball."   c. "Floating on the Moon."

   b. "Six Hoops."   d. "Gravity and the Moon."

2. A fact is something true. An opinion is what you think. What answer is a fact?

   a. There are six basketball hoops on the moon.

   b. There is less gravity on the moon than there is on Earth.

   c. It would be more fun to play basketball on the moon than on Earth.

   d. People should be able to jump higher on Earth.

3. Earth and the moon would have the same gravity if

   a. Earth was bigger.

   b. the moon was smaller.

   c. Earth and the moon were the same size.

   d. no one jumped or played basketball.

Try this! Have one student go to the front of the class. Measure how far he/she jumps. Now measure six times farther! Show how far they would have jumped if they had been on the moon!

Show how far you could jump if you were on the moon! Color in the correct amount of boxes.

Earth ☐	Distance: _____ inches
Moon ☐ ☐ ☐ ☐ ☐ ☐ ☐ ☐ ☐ ☐ ☐	Distance: _____ inches

Name: _____

Why the Moon Gets Big and Small

Hungry Cat went to Bird's house. Hungry Cat said, "I am very hungry. Bird, you must feed me, or I will eat you!"

Bird did not have any food. If Bird told Hungry Cat he did not have any food, Hungry Cat would eat him. Bird picked up the moon. "Here," Bird said, "Eat this cheese."

Hungry Cat said, "Yummy, yummy!" Then, Hungry Cat tried to eat the moon. Slowly, slowly she put her mouth over the big, round moon. Then Hungry Cat had a problem. The moon did not fit in her stomach. Out it came! Hungry Cat did not give up. Over and over, Hungry Cat tried to eat the moon. Every time, the moon was too big to keep down.

1. In the story, if the moon is getting smaller in the sky, then

    a. Hungry Cat is trying to eat it.

    b. it is in Hungry Cat's stomach.

    c. Bird is picking it up.

    d. it came out of Hungry Cat's stomach.

2. What happens first in the story?

    a. Bird picked up the moon.

    b. Hungry Cat tried to eat the moon.

    c. Hungry Cat went to Bird's house.

    d. Bird did not have any food.

3. This story is fiction. It is a made-up story, but it was written to tell why something happens. It tells

    a. why the moon seems to get bigger and smaller in the sky.

    b. why cats have small stomachs.

    c. why the sun rises and sets.

    d. why the moon is made of cheese.

Name: _____

New Life Form Report

Dear Sir:

My report on the new life form is below. In all my space travels, I have never seen anything like it.

REPORT

How they move: They seem to be missing legs. They only have four. They walk on two. The other two they use to grab things.

How they talk: Very strange. They make noises with a hole that is in a ball on top of their bodies.

How they see: They only have two eyes! They cannot see all the way around. They can only see in front of themselves!

Color: It is hard to say, Sir. They are changing their skin and color all the time! Sometimes, they take off their skin when they go inside.

Where they live: I found them on a strange planet with lots of liquid. The liquid is often called "water."

1. The two legs that could "grab things" were most likely

   a. arms with feet.

   b. arms with hands.

   c. arms with eyes.

   d. arms with holes at the end.

2. How might the new life forms be "changing their skin color" when they go inside?

   a. They grab something with their legs.

   b. They write a report.

   c. They talk strangely.

   d. They take off their coats.

3. Why might the new life form be a human?

   a. They live on a planet with water.

   b. They live on a planet with two suns.

   c. They can travel in space.

   d. They use their eyes to see all the way around.

Name: _____

Taller, Taller, Shorter

A boy and a girl grow. They grow tall. They grow taller and taller. Days go by. Months go by. Years go by. After many years, the boy and girl are all grown up. They are big people now. They are adults. They are done growing. The boy is now a man. The girl is now a woman.

Then one day the man measures himself. He is two inches taller! The woman measures herself, too. She has grown two inches, too. How can adults grow taller? What is going on?

The man and the woman are astronauts. In space, the astronauts float. Gravity does not pull them down. The astronauts' spines stretch because there is no gravity. The astronauts grow taller. Back on Earth, the astronauts shrink back to their normal height. It takes several months for them to return to their normal height.

1. When something grows *smaller*, it

   a. shrinks.   **b.** floats.   **c.** pulls.   **d.** measures.

2. Why do the astronauts float in space?

   a. They are growing.

   b. They are adults.

   c. Years go by.

   d. There is no gravity.

3. How long does it take for an astronaut to shrink back to his or her normal height?

   a. several days

   b. a day and a month

   c. several months

   d. years

4. This story is mainly about

   a. adults.

   b. the height of astronauts.

   c. how to measure.

   d. gravity on Earth.

Name: _____

Strange Salt, Strange Pepper

"Where is the salt? Where is the pepper? I can't find them. I want salt and pepper to put on my food! Where is the salt and pepper? I want to sprinkle salt and pepper on my food."

"Here it is," Robot said. Robot handed the new astronaut two bottles. The new astronaut was ready to eat. His tray was strapped to his lap.

The new astronaut groaned. "This can't be salt. This can't be pepper. These bottles are filled with liquid. Salt and pepper are not wet."

Robot said, "In space, you mix the salt in water. The pepper is in oil. The salt and pepper have to be liquid. The liquid is in a squeeze bottle. This stops pieces of salt and pepper from floating in the air."

Robot watched the astronaut squeeze pepper onto his food. Robot said, "I will never understand why humans eat pepper. Oil is best! Why do humans make oil bad by putting pepper in it? Humans are strange!"

1. Most likely, the new astronaut strapped his tray to his lap

   a. so he could sprinkle salt on it.

   b. so Robot could find it.

   c. so he could sprinkle pepper on it.

   d. so it would not float away.

2. What might happen if the salt and pepper were not liquid?

   a. The oil would get too dry.

   b. The astronauts would eat too much.

   c. A piece of pepper could get in an astronaut's eye.

   d. All the food would have to be put in squeeze bottles.

3. Most likely, the astronaut

   a. had never been to space before.

   b. had been to space many times.

   c. had never eaten salt before.

   d. had never eaten pepper before.

4. What type of oil does Robot like?

   a. oil with salt in it

   b. oil with nothing in it

   c. oil with pepper in it

   d. oil that isn't liquid

Name: _____

Write On!

You are an astronaut. You are writing a report on what you see and do. In your report, you must include information from the stories you read. For example, tell how high you jump, what you eat, or how things are different in space. You can make up things, too! Imagine whom you might see or meet! What do your new friends look like?

_____

_____

_____

_____

_____

_____

_____

_____

_____

_____

_____

_____

_____

_____

_____

_____

Name: _____

Suitcase Surprise

Stop! Something was wrong! The agent said, "There is something wrong. You must open your suitcase. We have to see what is in your suitcase."

Jill was at the airport. She had to put her suitcase through a scanner. When Jill's suitcase was in the scanner, it triggered an alarm. She was surprised. What was in her suitcase that could trigger an alarm? Jill had packed clothes. She had packed two books. She had packed her toothbrush. None of those things should make an alarm go off. What could be wrong?

The agent opened Jill's suitcase. The agent was surprised, and Jill was, too. Jill's dog had crawled into her suitcase! Jill said, "He must have crawled under my clothes when I went to get my toothbrush!"

1. From reading the story, it appears that Jill did **not** pack

   a. a shirt.

   b. a dress.

   c. a pair of pants.

   d. a hairbrush.

2. This story is mainly about

   a. dogs.

   b. why an alarm was triggered.

   c. suitcases.

   d. what Jill packed.

3. Most likely, Jill's dog is

   a. the same size as a cat.

   b. the same size as a suitcase.

   c. the same size as a mouse.

   d. the same size as a chair.

Name: _____

Rules, Rules, Rules

Rule number one: No talking.

Rule number two: No moving.

Rule number three: No sneezing.

Rule number four: No smiling.

People had to follow these rules for 15 minutes. Why were these rules made? Today, we can snap a picture. It is easy and fast. We have good cameras. Old cameras were not as fast. They were slow. People had to stay still for 15 minutes! If they moved, the picture would be ruined.

It is very hard to stay still for 15 minutes. It is easier to stay still if you don't smile. Try it. You will see. Smiling takes muscles. Fifteen minutes is too long to smile. Your muscles will need a rest.

1. A better title for this story might be

   a. "All About Muscles."

   b. "School Rules."

   c. "Taking Photos with Old Cameras."

   d. "Why Smiling Is Bad."

2. If you *snap* a picture, you

   a. ruin it.

   b. don't smile.

   c. need a rest.

   d. take it.

3. Most likely, the author thinks that

   a. new cameras are better than old cameras.

   b. it is too hard to smile.

   c. it is easy to stay still for 15 minutes.

   d. we need more rules today.

Name: _____

The Bone Proof

The Daily News

January 19   1896

THE BONE PROOF

By George Smith

Eddie McCarthy fell yesterday. Eddie is ten years old. He was skating on the ice. Eddie hurt his wrist. It hurt a lot. Eddie was in a lot of pain. Eddie's parents were worried. Was Eddie's wrist broken? They could not tell.

Eddie's parents took him to the doctor. The doctor proved Eddie's wrist was broken. How did he do this? He used a new invention. He used a machine that took an x-ray. The x-ray took a photo of Eddie's bones!

This new machine is a great invention. It will help people. Doctors will now know if bones are broken. Doctors can take pictures to prove it!

1. When you *prove* something, you must

   a. make a machine.

   b. show that it is true.

   c. break it.

   d. use an invention.

2. Why was the x-ray machine a great invention?

   a. People could write stories about it.

   b. It helped doctors know if bones were broken.

   c. It could make people feel a lot of pain.

   d. It stopped parents from worrying.

3. When a person is *in pain*, that person

   a. takes a picture.

   b. is skating.

   c. invents something.

   d. hurts.

 #8123 *Let's Get This Day Started: Reading*   ©*Teacher Created Resources*

Name: _____

Apple Picking

"I need all the apples picked today," Ellie and Ben's mother said. "You must pick the apples before you go play." Ellie and Ben picked all the apples close to the ground. The low apples were easy to reach. The low apples were all picked, but there were still a lot of apples on the tree. The unpicked apples were high up. They were on the top branches.

Ellie and Ben got their jet packs. They put them on. They flew up to the top of the tree. They flew from high branch to high branch. They picked all the apples. Soon, they had picked every apple.

"Long ago, people did not have jet packs," Ellie said. "How did they pick apples? Did the apples at the top of the trees go to waste?"

"They did not have jet packs," Ben said. "They had something else. They had ladders."

When Ellie heard that, she started to laugh. "That's funny!" she said. "No one needs a ladder today."

1. How do you know this story did not take place in the past?
   a. In the past, no one needed to pick apples.
   b. In the past, apple trees did not have high branches.
   c. In the past, people let apples go to waste.
   d. In the past, no one had jet packs.

2. What happened first in the story?
   a. Ellie and Ben put on jet packs.
   b. Ellie and Ben picked the low apples.
   c. Ben told Ellie that people used ladders.
   d. Ben told Ellie people did not have jet packs.

3. Why did the people use ladders?
   a. so they could reach the apples on the high branches
   b. so they could reach the apples on the low branches
   c. so they could reach the apples close to the ground
   d. so they could reach the apples on the ground

4. If good fruit is not used, it
   a. is yummy.   b. is funny.   c. goes to waste.   d. is very high.

Name: _____

Writing Dots

How many books are in your school? Long ago, Louis Braille went to a school where there were only 14 books. Only 14 books in the whole school! The books were very big. They were very heavy.

Louis could not see. He was blind. He went to a special school for blind children. The books in the school had raised print. He had to feel the letters with his fingers. The books were hard to read. It took a long time to feel all the letters.

A man came to Louis's school. He told all the children about a code. The code was made of raised dots. People could feel the dots. Then, they could read the message even in the dark.

Louis was just a boy, but he thought, "I can make a better code. My code will help blind people read fast. They will not need heavy books with big raised letters. They can have small books with small raised dots."

Today, there are lots of books for blind people. These books are all written in Braille. They all have raised dots for letters.

1. Louis first thought of Braille when he

   a. was a boy.

   b. was a man.

   c. had to read a message at night.

   d. was done with school.

2. One can feel the dots in Braille because

   a. they are big.   b. they are a code.   c. they are heavy.   d. they are raised.

3. This story was written so you could

   a. learn about the man who came to Louis's school.

   b. think about how many books are in your school.

   c. learn about different codes.

   d. learn how Braille books were invented for blind people.

4. Most likely, a person would feel the raised dots with his or her

   a. hands.   b. mouth.   c. fingers.   d. arms.

Name: _____

Write On!

Think about long ago. Think about today. Think about what might happen in the future. Now, think about what has already been invented. Think about what might be invented one day.

In the space below, write down how some things have changed over time. Use an example from the past and present. Tell how the world might be different in the future. When you write, use some of the information from the stories in order to help you.

_____

_____

_____

_____

_____

_____

_____

_____

_____

_____

_____

_____

_____

Name: _____

What Am I?

I have four legs. I have a tail. I have four legs and a tail, but I do not bark. What animal has four legs, a tail, and does not bark? Could it be a cat?

Yes, I am a cat, but what kind of cat? I have claws. My claws stay out. I cannot retract them. I cannot bring them back in. I am the only cat that has claws that will not retract. I am the only cat whose claws do not go in and out.

Why do my claws stay out? They help me go fast. They stop me from slipping. They help make me the fastest cat. I am a cheetah!

1. When something is *retracted*, it

    a. is taken back.

    b. is pushed up.

    c. goes down.

    d. stays out.

2. Why do a cheetah's claws stay out?

    a. to help it bark

    b. to scare other animals

    c. to help it dig holes

    d. to help stop it from slipping when it is running

3. The author wrote this story

    a. so you could learn about dogs.

    b. so you could learn about cheetahs.

    c. so you could learn how to be fast.

    d. so you could learn about dog claws.

Name: _____

Sad People

I feel sorry for people. They must be sad. They have to be sad! I would be sad if I only had one heart. How strange to think that people have only one heart! I am happy because I have three hearts.

I feel sorry for people. They must be sad. They have to be sad! I would be sad if I had red blood. How strange to think that people have red blood! I am happy because I have blue blood.

I feel sorry for people. They must be sad. They have to be sad! I would be sad if I only had two arms. How strange to think that people have only two arms. I am happy because I have eight arms! I have three hearts, blue blood, and eight arms because I am an octopus. I am very happy that I am an octopus!

1. How is an octopus different from people?

   a. An octopus has two arms.

   b. An octopus has red blood.

   c. An octopus has one heart.

   d. An octopus has more arms.

2. Who is telling the story?

   a. people

   b. sad people

   c. an octopus

   d. three octopuses

3. Another name for this story might be

   a. "The Strange Octopus."

   b. "What the Octopus Feels."

   c. "The Sad Octopus."

   d. "Three Happy Hearts."

Name: _____

Clues

A clue is a hint. How many clues do you need before you can correctly guess the animal?

Clue 1: I have one heart. My heart is big. How long is my heart? It is two feet long! How much does my heart weigh? It weighs 25 pounds!

Clue 2: You have seven bones in your neck. I have seven bones in my neck, too! Are my seven bones the same size as yours? No, my neck bones are a lot bigger than yours.

Clue 3: I only need to drink water every couple of days.

Clue 4: How old am I when I can first run? I can run when I am only one hour old!

Clue 5: When I am born, I drop five feet to the ground! Ouch!

What am I? Do you know yet? I am the tallest animal. I am a giraffe!

1. A fact is something true. What answer is a fact?

   a. I think giraffes are pretty.

   b. Giraffes should drink more water.

   c. A giraffe has seven neck bones.

   d. Giraffes are better than cheetahs.

2. What do you learn from Clue 4?

   a. how old a giraffe is when it can run

   b. how big a giraffe's heart is

   c. how far a giraffe drops when it is born

   d. how often a giraffe drinks water

3. Why wasn't the title of the story "The Giraffe"?

   a. The story is about many kinds of animals.

   b. The story is mostly about a giraffe's heart.

   c. It would not be as much fun to read because you would already know what animal it is.

   d. If you didn't like giraffes, you would not read the story.

Name: _____

What Reptile?

Reptiles are a kind of animal. You are a kind of animal, but you are not a reptile. You have hair. You are warm-blooded. You do not lay eggs. When you are a baby, you drink milk.

You see one kind of reptile with its mouth open. What kind of reptile is it? Why is its mouth open? The reptile is hot. It cannot sweat. You cool down by sweating. This reptile cools down by keeping its mouth open!

This kind of reptile has excellent hearing. It lays eggs. It can hear its babies crying inside the eggs! What kind of reptile can it be?

This kind of reptile does not chew its food. It tears off huge chunks. It swallows the big pieces. Then, it can go a long time without eating. The chunks must be very big pieces because sometimes this reptile can go more than a year without eating! What reptile is this? It is a crocodile!

1. Most likely, when would you see a crocodile with its mouth open?

   a. on a rainy day

   b. on a very hot day

   c. after the sun has set

   d. on a cool day

2. If an animal has *excellent* hearing,

   a. it has poor hearing.

   b. it lays eggs.

   c. it can hear well.

   d. it is a reptile.

3. If you ate a big piece of apple, you

   a. are a reptile.

   b. drink milk.

   c. do not need to eat for a year.

   d. ate a chunk.

4. This story is mainly about

   a. animals with hair.

   b. one kind of reptile.

   c. animals without hair.

   d. all kinds of reptiles.

Name: _____

Not Strange

A gallon is a lot. I can drink 40 gallons of water at a time! This may be strange to you. It is not strange to me. It helps me survive. It helps me live where it is hot and dry. It helps me live where water is hard to find. It helps me live in the desert.

I breathe through my nose. I breathe in and out. I breathe air in and out of my nostrils. I can close my nostrils. I can shut them. This may be strange to you. It is not strange to me. It helps me survive. It helps me keep sand out of my nose when the wind blows.

Do you know what I am? I am a camel. Some camels have one hump. Another kind of camel has two humps. Our humps can get big. Other times they get small. This may be strange to you. It is not strange to me. We store fat in our humps. The stored fat helps us survive. When we do not eat for days and days, we use the fat in our humps to survive. As we use the fat, our humps get smaller and smaller. Our humps will get big again when we eat and drink.

1. When something *survives*,

   a. it lives.   b. it is strange.   c. it has a hump.   d. it gets big.

2. If a camel drinks 40 gallons of water,

   a. its hump will get smaller.

   b. its hump will stay the same.

   c. its hump will get bigger.

   d. its one hump will become two humps.

3. This story is mainly about

   a. how many humps a camel has.

   b. a camel's nostrils.

   c. the desert.

   d. what helps a camel survive.

4. What do camels store in their humps?

   a. air   b. fat   c. water   d. food

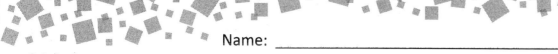

Name: _____

Write On!

Look back at the story titled "Clues." Think of any animal but the giraffe. Write a story about your animal. If you want, it can be one of the animals from the stories in this unit. Write your story just like the "Clues" story. Make the first clues hard. Make the last clues easy.

Clue 1: _____

_____

_____

Clue 2: _____

_____

_____

Clue 3: _____

_____

_____

Clue 4: _____

_____

_____

Clue 5: _____

_____

_____

Read your story to the class. Afterward, see if people can guess your animal.

Name: _____

Fairy Tale

Some stories are made up. They are not real. A story may take place in a land that is not real. It is an imaginary place. It may have animals that are not real. They are imaginary animals. It may have people that are not real. They are imaginary people.

The story may have dragons. The dragons may like gold. The story may have a princess. The princess may sleep for a hundred years. The story may have a giant. The giant may have a magic hen. What kind of story is this? It is a fairy tale!

One fairy tale is about a princess. She is locked in a tower. The tower is tall. It has no stairs. It does not have a door. How does a prince get up into the tower? The princess has long hair. The prince climbs up the princess's hair!

1. When something is *imaginary*

   a. it is locked in a tower.

   b. it is a very long story.

   c. it is not real.

   d. it is about a tall tower.

2. Another title for this story might be

   a. "The Dragon in the Tower."

   b. "A Kind of Story."

   c. "True Stories."

   d. "Why Long Hair Is Best."

3. What animal below would most likely be found in a fairy tale?

   a. a horse that can fly

   b. a brown horse

   c. a horse you can ride

   d. a horse that can run fast

Name: _____

Silly and Smarty

Silly Tilly said, "I like riddles. Smarty Arty, I am going to ask you a riddle. What has to be broken before you can use it?"

Smarty Arty thought and thought. Then he said, "I know! I know what you have to break before you can use it. It is an egg!"

Silly Tilly said, "What has a thumb and four fingers, but it is not alive?" Once again, Smarty Arty thought and thought. Once again he knew the answer. He knew a glove had four fingers and a thumb.

Silly Tilly said, "You have something. It is yours. You cannot lend it. No one can borrow it. Sometimes it is big. Sometimes it is small. Sometimes you don't have it at all. What is it?"

Smarty Arty didn't have to think for a long time. He thought of the answer right away. "My shadow!" he said.

1. How many riddles are in the story?

   a. two   **b.** three   **c.** four   **d.** five

2. Most likely, what is the answer to this riddle: *What goes up but can't go down?*

   a. a book

   b. your hair

   c. a bike

   d. your age

3. What will Silly Tilly likely say next?

   a. an answer to a riddle

   b. a math problem

   c. a riddle

   d. a sad story

Name: _____

A Special Kind of Joke

A joke is a funny story. It is told to amuse someone or to make him or her laugh. The line in the story that surprises you and makes you laugh is called the *punch line*. Usually the punch line is the last line of the joke.

One kind of joke is called a *knock-knock* joke. One example of a knock-knock joke goes like this:

Knock, knock.
Who's there?
Lettuce.
Lettuce who?
Lettuce in! It's freezing out here!

The punch line is "Lettuce in! It's freezing out here!" That line makes you laugh because you were not expecting it. When you first hear the word *lettuce*, you do not think, "Let us." You think of a green leafy vegetable!

Here is another example of a knock-knock joke:

Knock, knock.
Who's there?
Cows go.
Cows go who?
No, silly. Cows go "moo!"

1. What is the punch line of this joke?

   Knock, knock.
   Who's there?
   Boo Hoo.
   Boo Hoo who?
   Don't cry! It's just a joke!

   a. the first line
   b. the second line
   c. the fourth line
   d. the fifth line

2. This story is mainly about

   a. knock-knock jokes.
   b. three kinds of jokes.
   c. what makes a good punch line.
   d. what cows say.

3. When something makes you laugh, it

   a. hurts you.
   b. is an example.
   c. amuses you.
   d. can only be a knock-knock joke.

Name: _____

The Princess and the Pea

Hans Christian Andersen was a writer. He wrote fairy tales. One fairy tale he wrote was about a princess and a pea. In the fairy tale, a prince wanted to marry a real princess. The prince said no one else would be good enough. The prince looked all over, but he could not find a real princess. He was very sad.

One rainy night, there was a knock on the castle door. It was a girl. She was all wet. She was in rags. Still, she said she was a real princess. The queen said, "We shall see." The queen put a pea on a mattress. Then, she put 20 more mattresses on the pea! She put 20 quilts on top, too! The girl slept on top of all the mattresses and quilts.

In the morning the girl said, "I did not sleep well. I think there was a huge rock in my bed!" Then, the queen said that the girl was a real princess. She knew because only a real princess could feel the pea. The prince married the princess. They all lived happily ever after.

1. What happened first?

   a. The queen put twenty mattresses on the pea.

   b. A girl knocked on the castle door.

   c. The prince looked all over for a real princess.

   d. The queen said that the girl was a real princess.

2. What would Hans Christian Andersen most likely agree with?

   a. You should always sleep on twenty mattresses.

   b. You should always sleep on twenty quilts.

   c. You can tell who someone is by how they look.

   d. You can't tell who someone is by how they look.

3. Most likely, Hans Christian Andersen wrote this fairy tale to make you feel

   a. happy.   b. sad.   c. angry.   d. sleepy.

4. If someone really slept on twenty mattresses and twenty quilts, what might they need to get into bed?

   a. a car   b. a ladder   c. a blanket   d. a toothbrush

Name: _____

The Other Princess

Once upon a time, on a dark and rainy night, there was a knock on a castle door. The prince said, "Who can that be? No one should be out on a cold, wet night like this!"

A girl was at the door. She said, "I am a real princess. I want dry clothes. I want a warm bed. I want a prince to marry." The queen got a bed ready for the girl. First, she put a pea on a mattress. Next, she put twenty mattresses on top of the pea. Then she put twenty quilts on top of the mattresses.

In the morning, the queen asked the girl how she slept. "Horrible!" the girl cried. "Horrible!" she complained. "I barely slept a wink. I tossed. I turned. I think that there was a huge rock in my bed. I have never had such a horrible night in my life."

The prince said, "She may be a princess, but she is horrible! She is rude and spoiled. She never thanked us for taking her in. She never thanked us for giving her a warm, dry place to sleep. I am not the prince for her!"

1. Why did the prince think the girl was rude and spoiled?

   a. She complained and didn't thank them.

   b. She slept on twenty mattresses.

   c. She knocked on the castle door.

   d. She was out in the rain.

2. You are **not** told in the story

   a. how many mattresses the girl slept on.

   b. what the girl wanted.

   c. why the girl was out on a cold, wet night.

   d. where the queen put the pea.

3. Most likely, if your mattress was on a pea,

   a. you would not be able to sleep.

   b. you would have a horrible night.

   c. you would feel as though there was a huge rock in your bed.

   d. you would not know it.

4. If something is *horrible*,

   a. it is not huge.   b. it is not nice.   c. it is not cold.   d. it is not rainy.

Name: _____

Write On!

Time to write part of a fairy tale!

Think of two imaginary people or animals. Tell when and how they meet. Then, have one of them tell the other a riddle or a joke. What does the person or animal think of the joke?

If you want, you can use one of the riddles or jokes from the stories you just read.

_____

_____

_____

_____

_____

_____

_____

_____

_____

_____

_____

_____

_____

Name: _____

Where in the World?

It is May 25th. The sun is out. The day is over, but the sun does not set. The sun stays up for days and days. It never gets dark. The sun does not set until July 25th! It is light for two months! Where in the world does this happen? What country is it?

It is the middle of March. People come to play golf. The people do not play golf on grass. There is no grass. The people play golf on ice! They hit the ball with their clubs over ice fields. The players can see icebergs as they play. Where in the world can this be? What country is it?

The country is Greenland. Greenland is the world's biggest island. Almost all of Greenland is covered in ice.

1. From the story, you can tell that Greenland is most likely a

    a. cold country.

    b. warm country.

    c. hot country.

    d. very hot country.

2. The people in the story do not play golf

    a. on an island.

    b. on ice.

    c. in a country.

    d. on grass.

3. In Greenland, how long can it stay light?

    a. two days

    b. two weeks

    c. two months

    d. two years

Name: _____

A Place to Love

I love my home. I live on an island. It is the world's fourth-largest island. It is not the biggest island, but it is the best island. The name of my island is Madagascar.

I like the *baobab* trees on my island. They have huge trunks. When it rains, the tree draws up water with its roots. It stores the water in its big trunk. Some trees can store 26,000 (twenty-six thousand) gallons! When it is dry, the tree does not get thirsty. It uses the water in its trunk.

I live in a tree. I am a chameleon. I am a kind of lizard. I cannot store gallons of water, but I can do something else. I can change color! My skin can be blue. It can be green. It can be yellow or brown, too.

1. When something is *stored*, it
   a. is large.
   b. is saved.
   c. is thirsty.
   d. changes color.

2. When do you find out that a chameleon is telling the story?
   a. at the start of the second paragraph
   b. at the end of the second paragraph
   c. at the start of the last paragraph
   d. at the end of the last paragraph

3. What might be a better title for the story?
   a. "Lizards"
   b. "All About Trees"
   c. "Blue, Green, Yellow, or Brown"
   d. "Madagascar"

Name: _____

Letter to Grandpa

June 15

Dear Grandpa,

Every time I took a step today, I sank! Sometimes I sank down two inches. Sometimes I sank down four. Why did I sink? Why wasn't the ground hard and firm? I was on an island! The island was made of reeds! Reeds are plants. They get soft in the water. They rot. The people have to keep adding reeds to the top of their island.

I like this floating island! It is in a lake. It is in the country of Peru. We had to get to the island by boat. The boat was made of reeds, too! When the people cook here, they make a fire on stones. They have to bring the stones from the land. They cook lots of fish.

I will bring you something back from this island.

Love,

Maria

1. Most likely, the people use reeds to build their island and boats because

   a. there are not enough stones.

   b. the reeds rot in the water.

   c. a lot of reeds grow by the lake.

   d. they are in the country of Peru.

2. When something is *firm* it

   a. is soft.   b. is not soft.   c. floats.   d. does not float.

3. Most likely, the people cook on stones because

   a. the reeds would catch on fire.   c. the stones do not sink.

   b. the fish cannot eat the stones.   d. there are lots of stones on the island.

Name: _____

Down Under

Everyone says Greenland is the biggest island. I do not think so! No, no, no! I disagree. I think a different country is the largest island. What country am I thinking of? I will give you hints.

Hop, hop, hop! Kangaroos are hopping all across the land. Kangaroos have pouches. Kangaroo babies are called joeys. Mother kangaroos keep their joeys safe in their pouches. The joeys ride while their mothers hop!

Climb, climb, climb! Koalas are climbing all over the land. They climb high in trees. They sleep in the trees, too. When they are hungry, they eat the tree's leaves. Koalas have pouches, too. Baby koalas stay safe in their mothers' pouches.

Did the hints help? Did they help you know I was thinking of Australia? Australia is a continent. It is the smallest continent. It is an island, too. Why is it an island? It is all alone. It is not next to other countries. Water is all around it. It is an island continent!

1. The story does **not** tell you
   a. what a baby koala is called.
   b. what a baby kangaroo is called.
   c. where koalas sleep.
   d. where baby kangaroos stay safe.

2. The author wrote this story
   a. to make you disagree.
   b. to teach you about being safe.
   c. to tell you what she thinks.
   d. to tell you about Greenland.

3. A pocket is like a
   a. tree.   b. pouch.   c. baby.   d. continent.

4. Most likely, Greenland
   a. is surrounded by water.
   b. is very small.
   c. has kangaroos and koalas.
   d. is next to other countries.

Name: _____

The Silly Bridge

Olivia said, "Look at that silly bridge. No one can cross it! Its sides are too steep. There are no steps. Someone must have made a mistake. I came to Christmas Island to see interesting things. This bridge is not interesting. It is just silly."

Jay said, "Wait! Wait, and you will see!"

Olivia waited. She saw something. She looked and looked. She rubbed her eyes. Then she looked again. There were red crabs everywhere! They were coming out of the forest. Thousands of them! They covered the ground. They made the ground look like a red carpet. The crabs came to the bridge. They crawled up its sides. They did not need steps. They crawled across the top. They went down the other side. Then the crabs crawled to the ocean.

Jay said, "Every year the crabs migrate. They go to the ocean. Every year they come back. The bridge is not for people. It is for crabs. The bridge keeps the crabs safe from cars."

Olivia said, "That is very interesting. The bridge is not silly at all. The bridge keeps crabs safe when they migrate. It is a helpful bridge!"

1. This story is mainly about

   a. interesting things to see.

   b. what Jay thinks.

   c. a bridge for crabs.

   d. Christmas Island.

2. How did the crabs move?

   a. They crawled.   b. They ran.   c. They jumped.   d. They walked.

3. From the story, you can tell that if an animal *migrates*, it

   a. must cross a bridge.

   b. is always on an island.

   c. is safe in the ocean.

   d. goes away and comes back.

4. Why did the author say the crabs were like a red carpet?

   a. so you would think the story was silly

   b. so you could picture how many crabs there were

   c. so you would want a carpet the same color

   d. so you would know why the bridge didn't have steps

Name: _____

Write On!

Write a letter. Look back at what you have read to remind yourself how to write the date, greeting, and ending of a letter. You may write your letter to anyone you want.

Include in your letter some of the things you learned about islands while reading.

_____

_____

_____

_____

_____

_____

_____

_____

_____

_____

_____

_____

_____

_____

_____

_____

Name: _____

Mary's Lamb

Mary had a little lamb. It was her pet. Mary's brother told her she should bring her lamb to school. Mary did. Were the children calm? Was the lamb calm? No one was calm! Everyone got excited. Everyone laughed. Everyone wanted to play with the lamb. The teacher told Mary that she needed to follow the rules. No lambs at school! Mary needed to leave her lamb at home.

Mary brought her lamb to school a long time ago. A poem was written about that day from long ago. Today, the poem is a common nursery rhyme.

The school Mary went to was very small. It had only one room. You can still see the school today. You can still see where the lamb made the children laugh and play!

1. Think about *hot* and *cold*. How are they different? Find two words that are different in the same way that *hot* and *cold* are different.

   a. small and little

   b. calm and excited

   c. lamb and pet

   d. school and rule

2. This story is mainly about

   a. a nursery rhyme.

   b. brothers and sisters.

   c. how children play.

   d. a school for lambs.

3. What did the teacher tell Mary?

   a. Mary needed to follow the rules.

   b. Mary could bring her lamb to school.

   c. Mary could not laugh or play.

   d. Mary was excited to see the lamb.

Name: _____

Little Piggy

This little piggy went to market. This little piggy stayed home. This little piggy had roast beef. This little piggy had none. And this little piggy cried "Wee, wee, wee!" all the way home.

The big pigs in first grade said, "No." The big pigs said, "That is not the way we will do things. Who will go to the store? We all will! We will all find the roast beef. We will all bring the roast beef home. We will do it together."

The big pigs in first grade said, "We will all cook the roast beef. Then, we will all eat together. No one will be alone. No one will be hungry. We will help each other so that no one will cry!"

1. Each little piggy did a different thing. How many little pigs were there?

   a. three   **b.** four   **c.** five   **d.** six

2. From the story, you can tell that *going to the market* is like

   a. cooking roast beef.

   b. going to the store.

   c. crying all the way home.

   d. staying home.

3. How did the big first-grade pigs do things?

   a. They did them together.

   b. They did them hungry.

   c. They did them alone.

   d. They did them crying.

Name: _____

Jack and Jill

Jack said he was thirsty. He wanted a drink of water. He told Jill he was going to go up the hill to fetch a pail of water. Jill said she would go with him. She knew a bucket of water would be heavy, and she would help him carry it down.

Jack and Jill filled the pail with water. Together, they carried the heavy bucket down the hill. Suddenly, Jill cried, "Look! A cow is jumping over the moon!"

Jack said, "I won't look up! You are trying to trick me! Cows can't jump over the moon!" Then Jack said, "Look to the right. If you look to the right, you will see a dish running away with a spoon."

Jill started to laugh. She laughed so hard that she fell onto the ground. The bucket spilled, and both Jack and Jill tumbled down the hill. Over and over they rolled—all the way to the bottom. When they stopped, Jill said, "Look to the left. There is a drinking fountain! We can have a drink as soon as the cat with the fiddle has taken his turn."

1. The dish running away with the spoon was said to be

    a. up.

    b. down.

    c. to the left.

    d. to the right.

2. When you *tumble*, you

    a. are thirsty.

    b. fall down and roll.

    c. see a drinking fountain.

    d. help carry a heavy pail.

3. Jill might have said that she saw a cat with a fiddle because she

    a. was trying to trick Jack.

    b. wanted to help Jack.

    c. needed to fetch water.

    d. was at the bottom of the hill.

Name: _____

Where Was Tom?

Tom was missing! Where could he be? His mother went looking for him. She looked in his room. She looked all over the house. She went outside and looked in the yard. She could not find Tom anywhere.

Finally, Tom's mother found him. Tom was in the neighbor's barn! He was sitting on a nest. The nest was full of goose eggs. Why was Tom sitting on goose eggs? Tom had asked his mother why geese sit on their eggs. She told him that it was so the eggs would hatch. Tom was sitting on the goose eggs to make them hatch. He had sat for hours and hours waiting for the eggs to hatch.

Tom's full name was Thomas Edison. Tom invented many things. One of the things he invented was the light bulb. He also made the first sound recording. What did Tom record? What were the first words ever to come from a machine? Tom recorded a nursery rhyme. He said, "Mary had a little lamb." When people heard those words coming from a machine, they were amazed. They could not believe that a machine could talk!

1. Why was Tom in the neighbor's barn?

   a. He was waiting for his mother.

   b. He was inventing the light bulb.

   c. He wanted to record sounds.

   d. He wanted to make goose eggs hatch.

2. What machine **cannot** play recorded sound?

   a. phone   b. bike   c. television   d. computer

3. The first sound recording was of

   a. a book.   b. a song.   c. a nursery rhyme.   d. a riddle.

4. Most likely, when Tom sat on the eggs,

   a. the eggs hatched.

   b. he recorded what he was doing.

   c. he invented a machine to hatch eggs.

   d. he broke the eggs.

Name: _____

Hickory, Dickory, Dock

I'm sure you have heard the nursery rhyme about my two friends and me. It goes like this.

Hickory, Dickory, Dock,
The mouse ran up the clock.
The clock struck one,
The mouse ran down!
Hickory, Dickory, Dock.

I am going to tell you the truth. I am going to tell you why I ran up the clock. Hickory, Dickory, and I were playing hide-and-seek. It was my turn to hide, and I thought the clock was a perfect place to hide. No one would find me. I could stay hidden as long as I wanted.

The clock was a perfect place to hide. I waited and waited for someone to find me, but no one did. I waited so long that I fell asleep! The next thing I knew, I heard a big, loud sound! The clock had struck one! It woke me up, so I ran down. When I got down, Hickory and Dickory said, "Dock, where did you hide? We looked and looked, but we could not find you."

1. Why did Dock run up the clock?

   a. It was his turn to hide.

   b. It was a perfect place to sleep.

   c. He wanted to hear a big, loud sound.

   d. He knew Hickory and Dickory would look for him.

2. When do you find out the name of the mouse that went up the clock?

   a. when he says he is going to tell the truth

   b. at the start of the story, when Hickory and Dickory call him by name

   c. when he tells you his name

   d. at the end of the story, when Hickory and Dickory call him by name

3. If something is *perfect*, it is

   a. good.   b. sad.   c. bad.   d. hidden.

4. Who is telling the story?

   a. Hickory   b. Dickory   c. Dock   d. Hickory and Dickory

Name: _____

Write On!

Time to write a nursery rhyme! Finish the sentences below. Have the smart first grader do some of the things you just read about.

This smart first grader went _____

_____

_____.

This smart first grader stayed _____

_____

_____.

This smart first grader had _____

_____

_____.

This smart first grader played _____

_____

_____.

This smart first grader cried _____

_____

_____.

Name: _____

Hungry Ants

An ant is hungry. What does it do? You can store food in a refrigerator. You can keep food in a cupboard. When you are hungry, you go get the food you have saved. The ant does not have a refrigerator. It does not have a cupboard. Where can the ant store food? Where can it save food? The ant can store food in other ants!

There are many kinds of ants. One kind is the honeypot ant. Honeypot ants store food in other ants. Worker ants get food. They feed it to the storage ants. The bellies of the storage ants get big. They look like huge pots.

When the worker ants need food, they stroke the storage ants. When the storage ants are petted, they open their mouths. Out comes the stored food!

1. A better title for this story would be

    a. "Worker Ants."

    b. "Ants."

    c. "Storage Ants."

    d. "Honeypot Ants."

2. When something is *stroked*, it is

    a. fed.   **b.** petted.   **c.** saved.   **d.** stored.

3. From the story, you can tell that

    a. not all ants store food in other ants.

    b. there is only one kind of ant.

    c. all ants are worker ants.

    d. ants have pots to store food in.

Name: _____

Little and Big

Help! Ant fell into the water, and she was being carried away. Ant kicked her six legs over and over, but she could not make it to the shore.

Dove saw Ant struggling in the water. Feeling sorry for Ant, Dove threw a stick into the water. Ant grabbed on to the stick and was able to make it to shore. Ant said, "I will be your friend," but Dove just laughed. Dove told Ant she was too little to be a friend.

The next day Dove was on the ground eating seeds. Ant saw a man with a net creeping up on Dove. Ant crawled up the man's leg and bit him hard! Dove flew away when she heard the man shout "Ouch!" Then Dove said to Ant, "You are little, but you are a big friend."

1. If you are *struggling*, you

   a. are very little.

   b. can't hear someone creeping.

   c. are having a hard time getting something done.

   d. are able to make it to shore.

2. What can students learn from the story?

   a. Size does not matter.

   b. It is better to be big.

   c. No one needs to help.

   d. It is good to laugh.

3. Why did Dove throw a stick to Ant?

   a. Dove wanted to be Ant's friend.

   b. Dove was bigger than Ant.

   c. Ant bit the man for Dove.

   d. Dove felt sorry for Ant.

Name: _____

Book Report

The Sting of the Wild is a good book. It is a true story. It was written by Justin O. Schmidt.

Justin studies insects. He has been stung by many insects. Sometimes Justin does not want to get stung. Other times, he gets stung on purpose. Justin has been stung more than 83 times!

Not all insect stings hurt. Some hurt a lot! Justin has made a scale. The scale tells how much a sting hurts. The scale goes from one to four. If the sting is a one, it doesn't hurt a lot. If the sting is a four, it hurts a lot!

I think everyone should read this book. It is fun to read what Justin says about the different insect stings. Justin said that the bullet ant sting was a four. He said the bullet ant sting hurts as much as walking on fire!

1. An insect stings you. You don't know it. On Justin's scale, it is most likely a

    a. one.   **b.** two.   **c.** three.   **d.** four.

2. An insect stings you. It hurts so much that you want to cry! On Justin's scale, it is most likely a

    a. one.   **b.** four.   **c.** six.   **d.** seven.

3. When does the book report writer tell you that you should read the book?

    a. after she tells you about the bullet ant

    b. before she tells you the book is true

    c. before she tells you how many times Justin was stung

    d. after she tells you how the scale works

Name: _____

Not a Spider

Most people think spiders are insects. Spiders are not insects. Spiders have eight legs. Insects only have six legs. Spiders do not have antennae on their heads. Insects have antennae on their heads. Spiders eat mostly insects. Insects eat all kinds of things. Spiders never have wings. Many insects have wings.

Some insects live in colonies. A colony is made up of many insects. The insects work together. There is a queen. The queen lays eggs. There are workers. The workers gather food. They feed the queen, too. Some ants are soldier ants. The soldier ants protect the colony. They help to keep the other ants safe.

Ants are insects. There are many kinds of ants. Ants are small, but they are very strong for their size. Ants can lift more than their own weight. What could you pick up if you were as strong as an ant? You could pick up a car!

Some ants are farmers. They grow their own food. The ants cut leaves. They carry the leaves home. They chew the leaves and spit them out. Fungus grows on the spit-out leaves. The ants eat the fungus that grows on the chewed-up leaves.

1. What answer is true?

    a. Ants can pick up cars.

    b. Spiders do not have antennae.

    c. Insects do not have wings.

    d. Spiders have six legs.

2. This story is mainly about

    a. spiders.   b. farmer ants.   c. insects.   d. colonies.

3. What kind of ant gathers food?

    a. the queen ant   b. the soldier ant   c. the spider ant   d. the worker ant

4. What do the farmer ants do third?

    a. They chew the leaves and spit them out.

    b. They cut the leaves.

    c. They eat the fungus on the leaves.

    d. They carry the leaves home.

Name: _____

Grasshopper and Ant

Grasshopper was having fun. He was hopping, chirping, and singing. Then, Grasshopper saw Ant. Ant was carrying some corn. The corn was heavy and hard to carry. "Ant, give up! Stop working so hard! Come hop and chirp and sing with me!" Grasshopper said.

Ant would not stop working. As he carried the heavy piece of corn he said, "I cannot stop. I am storing up food for winter. You should do the same."

Grasshopper laughed. He said, "Why bother about the future? It is the present. We have plenty of food right now. There is no need to worry about the future. Now is the time to be having fun."

Days passed. Summer ended. The days got shorter, and the air turned cold. All the trees lost their leaves. Snow fell and covered the ground. Grasshopper could not find food. "Oh, dear," he said. "I should have been like Ant. If I had thought about the future, I would have stored up food. I have learned that it is best to work hard in the present and save up for the future."

1. What did Grasshopper think about at the beginning of the story?

    a. It was the time to store food.   **c.** It was the time to have fun.

    b. It was the time to save up.   **d.** It was the time to work hard.

2. What activity are you more likely to do in the future, but not today?

    a. eat dinner   **c.** drive a car

    b. play with a friend   **d.** read a book

3. At the end of the story, the days were

    a. warmer.   **c.** longer.

    b. colder.   **d.** covered in leaves.

4. Most likely, what did Ant do with the corn he was carrying?

    a. He ate it when snow covered the ground.

    b. He put it down so he could hop, chirp, and sing.

    c. He ate it when there was plenty of food.

    d. He put it down because it was so hard to carry.

Name: _____

Write On!

Choose your favorite story from this unit. Write a book report about the story. Make sure to include what the story is about and whether or not you think other people will enjoy it. You may not write about *Book Report*, but you may use it as an example.

> **Sentence 1:** What is the title of the story?
>
> **Sentence 2:** Is the story true or not true?
>
> **Sentences 3 and 4:** What is the story about?
>
> **Sentence 5:** Do you think other people should read this book? Why?

_____

_____

_____

_____

_____

_____

_____

_____

_____

_____

_____

_____

Name: _____

A Kind of Boat

An outrigger is a kind of boat. It is like a canoe, but it has one or two floats. The floats are attached to the canoe's sides. The floats are known as outriggers. What do the floats do? They help balance the canoe. They help keep it balanced when the waves are big and the water is rough.

Long ago, people paddled their outriggers. They paddled for many days. They looked up at the stars. The stars helped them know where they were going. They felt the waves. The movement of the water helped them know what direction they were going. The people found empty islands. Some of the people stayed on the islands. They made new homes there.

1. Why might an outrigger be better for a long trip than a canoe?

   a. In a storm, an outrigger would be less likely to tip over.

   b. In an outrigger, a person would not have to paddle.

   c. It would be easier to see the stars in an outrigger.

   d. During a storm, it would be easier to feel the waves in an outrigger.

2. What did people use to help them know where they were going?

   a. the stars only

   b. the waves only

   c. the movement of the water only

   d. the stars and the waves

3. A better title for this story might be

   a. "Finding New Islands."

   b. "How to Balance."

   c. "Outriggers."

   d. "Paddling."

Name: _____

Birthday Treat

It was Max's birthday. Max's uncle took him fishing as a birthday treat. Max and his uncle went out in a motorboat. They motored to the middle of a lake. They sat, gently rocking in the water.

The two fishermen put bait on their hooks. Then, they cast their lines into the water. They waited and waited. Finally, Max felt a tug on his line! He had caught something! Max pulled and pulled. "I have caught the biggest fish in the world," he thought. Max pulled and pulled some more. Finally, he could see what was on the end of his hook. It was not the biggest fish in the world. It was an old bicycle wheel!

1. How do you think Max felt when he saw what was on his line?

   a. glad   **b.** surprised   **c.** happy   **d.** scared

2. Before Max cast his line,

   a. he put bait on it.

   b. he pulled on it.

   c. he caught a bicycle wheel.

   d. he waited and waited.

3. This story is mainly about

   a. Max's uncle.

   b. how old Max was.

   c. Max's fishing trip.

   d. Max's birthday party.

Name: _____

Captain's Log

Log for the Fair Winds

Captain Margo   **May 15, 1569**

Passenger count: 102 (baby girl born last night to Mary Dodd)

Crew count: 30

Cabin boy Joe Smith's broken arm is healing.

Location: 5° north of the equator.

Sea is flat. No waves. We are in the part of the ocean they call the doldrums. The doldrums is known for calm days. Sailing ships can be trapped here for days and sometimes weeks.

Today marks our twelfth day of being stuck in the doldrums. There has not been one bit of wind to fill our sails. There is no sign of rain. We only have enough water left for one week. Only one cup of water will be given two times a day until it rains. I ordered seven of the crew to set out fishing lines. The rest of the crew mended sails and scrubbed the decks.

1. What does a sailing ship need in order to move?

   a. calm days

   b. wind to fill its sails

   c. passengers and crew

   d. rain

2. When something is *calm*, it is

   a. cold and windy.

   b. clean and scrubbed.

   c. wet and rainy.

   d. still and quiet.

3. Which answer is true?

   a. There were more passengers than crew.

   b. Joe Smith was a passenger.

   c. The passengers scrubbed the decks.

   d. The passengers set out fishing lines.

Name: _____

Kayaks

A kayak is a kind of boat. It is small and narrow. It is for just one or two people. A paddle is used to make the boat go. The paddle is long and has two sides. A person dips one side in the water, and then they dip the other. The first kayaks were made a long time ago—almost 4,000 years! They were made by people who lived in the cold north.

The first kayaks were made with seal skin. The seal skin was stitched together. It was stretched over a frame. Some of the frames were made of wood. Other frames were made of whalebone.

Why were some frames wooden? Why were other frames made of bone? In the cold north, it is snowy and icy. It is hard for trees to grow. People used what they could find or hunt.

How long were the first kayaks? Stretch your arms out. Measure from fingertip to fingertip. Your kayak would be about three times the length of your outstretched hands. How wide would you make the hole to sit in? Measure your hips. Add two fists. Make the hole that size.

1. From the story, you can tell that
   a. trees only grow in the south.
   b. more seals live in the west than the east.
   c. whalebone is as strong as wood.
   d. some seals and whales live in the north.

2. A man stretches out his hands. It is six feet from fingertip to fingertip. How long should he make his kayak?
   a. 6 feet
   b. 6 + 6 feet
   c. 6 + 6 + 6 feet
   d. 6 + 6 + 6 + 6 feet

3. An engine makes a car go. A _____ makes a kayak go.
   a. paddle
   b. water
   c. wood
   d. frame

4. If something is *not wide*, it is
   a. made of whalebone.
   b. narrow.
   c. stretched.
   d. stitched.

Name: _____

The Largest Animal

Would they see it? Joy and Darren hoped they would. Joy and Darren wanted to see the largest animal in the world. They could not see the animal on land. It was not in a zoo. To see this animal, Joy and Darren had to ride on a boat. They had to go far out into the ocean.

The captain said, "Today is a good day for whale watching. I think you will see a blue whale. I looked at my old logs. Every year around this time, whales go by here. This is a good location for seeing whales."

The ocean was calm. It looked flat. Then Joy and Darren saw a big spray of water. It was a whale spouting! Then the whale came up out of the water. It was huge! They could see its back. They could see its tail. It was the biggest animal that Joy and Darren had ever seen. It was as long as two school buses!

Joy and Darren were very happy. They said, "We saw an animal whose tongue weighs as much as an elephant. We saw an animal whose heart weighs as much as a car. We saw a blue whale!"

1. Most likely, Joy and Darren

    a. were in an outrigger.   **c.** were in a sailing ship.

    b. were in a kayak.   **d.** were in a boat with a motor.

2. Why did the captain think they were in a good location to see whales?

    a. He had seen whales there before.

    b. They were far out in the ocean.

    c. The waves were spraying the boat.

    d. They could see two school buses.

3. What part of the blue whale weighs as much as a car?

    a. its tongue   **b.** its back   **c.** its heart   **d.** its tail

4. What did Joy and Darren see first?

    a. the whale's back   **c.** the whale's tail

    b. the whale spouting   **d.** the whale's head

Name: _____

Write On!

Write a Ship's Log. Look back at the story "Captain's Log" before you write. Include the same kinds of information. If you are the only one on the boat, then the passenger and crew count will be "0."

Make up a date. Then, write about what might happen on that day.

When you write, use information from the other stories. What kind of boat are you in? What is your location? What do you see? What do you do?

Log for the _____

Captain _____   Date: _____

Passenger Count: _____   Crew Count: _____

_____

_____

_____

_____

_____

_____

_____

_____

_____

_____

_____

_____

_____

Name: _____

Castle Stairs

Long ago, some people lived in castles. Knights helped keep the people in the castles safe. The stairs in the castles were not even. Some were high. Some were low. Why were the stairs uneven?

It is easy to trip on uneven steps. You can trip at night when there is little light and it is hard to see. You can trip during the day when you are not looking down or paying attention. The knights knew the stairs. They knew where they were high. They knew where they were low.

What if bad knights came to fight at the castle? They might trip on the stairs! The knights who were keeping the castle safe would not trip. They would know every high and every low step.

1. *Homophones* are words that sound the same. Two homophones in this story are

    a. knew and know.

    b. stairs and steps.

    c. knight and night.

    d. high and low.

2. A better title for this story is

    a. "Why Knights Fight."

    b. "Why Knights Should Pay Attention."

    c. "Why Uneven Stairs Are Bad."

    d. "Why Castles Were Made with Uneven Stairs."

3. The knights who lived at the castle were

    a. less likely to trip on the stairs.

    b. more likely to trip on the stairs.

    c. less likely to fight bad knights.

    d. more likely to fight bad knights.

Name: _____

The King's Sword

A magician said, "This sword is made of steel. The steel blade is strong and won't break." Then the magician said, "I am going to put this sword into a block of stone. That way no one can steal it. Only the real king will be able to pull out the steel sword."

Lots of knights tried to pull out the sword. Other people tried to steal it so they could be king. The sword remained stuck in the stone. Then one day a boy was helping a knight. The knight said, "I left my sword at the castle. Go quickly and get it for me."

The boy was rushing back to the castle when he saw the sword in the stone. "It will be quicker if I just borrow this sword," the boy said. He pulled on it, and out it came! The boy was the real king!

1. *Homophones* are words that sound the same. The two homophones in this story are

    a. steel and stone.

    b. steal and steel.

    c. steel and stuck.

    d. steal and sword.

2. Who put the sword in the stone?

    a. a boy   **b.** a knight   **c.** a magician   **d.** a king

3. Why did people want to steal the sword?

    a. They wanted people to think they were the real king.

    b. They wanted a sword that would not break.

    c. They did not want the boy to be king.

    d. They did not want to go all the way back to a castle.

Name: _____

A Note to My Reader

Do I like my job? Boys and girls ask me all the time. I am a writer. I write books for boys and girls, and yes, I like my job. I like it for many reasons.

The first reason is that I love words. I think words are playful. Think of words like *sea* and *see* or *blew* and *blue*. The words sound the same, but they do not mean the same. *Sun* and *son* and *aunt* and *ant* are fun words, too. When I write stories with these words, I feel as though I am playing with sound.

The second reason is that I am curious. I like to learn things. Before I write stories, I look up facts. I read about how things were long ago. I read stories about animals and all kinds of things. I also find out what is new in the world. I ask people questions. Then I put what I know into a story.

Sometimes, the story is nonfiction. Nonfiction stories are true. Sometimes, the story is not real. I make it up. Made-up stories are fiction stories. I have a lot of fun when I put facts in my fiction stories!

1. How many reasons does the author give for liking her job?

   a. one   **b.** two   **c.** three   **d.** four

2. What words might the author use if she feels as though she is playing with sound?

   a. shoe, foot   **c.** ate, eight

   b. fiction, true   **d.** real, true

3. If a story is *made up,* it is

   a. fiction.   **b.** true.   **c.** nonfiction.   **d.** real.

4. What answer is a fact about the author?

   a. I think she is a good writer.

   b. She asks questions.

   c. I like her nonfiction stories the best.

   d. She should write more stories.

Name: _____

Castle Windows

Look at an old castle that has not been rebuilt. It is made of stone. It is dark inside. There are not many windows to let in light. The windows do not have glass. Often, there are no low windows. There are no windows on the first floor! Do you know why there are not any windows on the first floor? The people in the castle wanted to be safe. People can climb in low windows. It is hard to climb in windows that are up high.

Some of the windows are slits. They are very long and narrow. They may be only two inches wide. People in the castle could shoot arrows out. It was easy to shoot an arrow out, but it was hard for an arrow to come in!

All of the windows are small, but some are bigger than slits. Still, very little light comes in. The windows are built with stone benches below them. What are the benches for? The benches are for people to sit on. Women can sit on the benches and sew. The light from the window helps them see what they are sewing.

1. *Homophon*es are words that sound the same. The two homophones in this story are

   a. know and no.

   b. sew and sewing.

   c. narrow and wide.

   d. see and sit.

2. From the story, you can tell that most likely old castles were dark because

   a. long ago the sun was not as bright.

   b. people did not turn on the lights.

   c. people liked the dark.

   d. of the way they were built.

3. Why were some of the windows narrow?

   a. to make it harder for an arrow to get in

   b. to make it so more light could come in

   c. to make it harder for an arrow to get out

   d. to make it so more light could get out

4. If an old castle were rebuilt, most likely

   a. all the windows would be made smaller.

   b. stones would be put in the windows.

   c. some bigger windows would be made into slits.

   d. some windows would be added and made bigger.

Name: _____

The Scary Sound

Dragon said, "I hear a sound. I do not like that sound. It is a scary sound. It scares me. I am not going to stay here. I will fly away." Dragon flapped his big wings. He rose into the air. Fire came out of his mouth as he flew away.

Dragon looked down while he was flying. He was afraid, but he was still curious. He wanted to know what was making the scary sound. "It will be worse if I don't know," Dragon said. Dragon turned around and flew back.

Dragon's heart beat faster. He felt it pounding against his chest. "I'll look for four seconds more," Dragon said to himself. "Then, I will turn around."

Dragon didn't have to look for four seconds. In two seconds, he saw what was making the scary sound. It was a baby dragon! The baby dragon had found a knight's helmet. Then he had tried to put the helmet on! Now, it was stuck. The baby dragon was crying because he couldn't get it off! The sound of his voice in the helmet was making the scary sound. "I'm glad I was curious," Dragon said as he helped the baby dragon take off the helmet.

1. A *homophone* is a word that sounds the same as another word. What homophones were **not** in the story?

    a. to, two   **b.** hear, here   **c.** for, four   **d.** be, bee

2. When you want to *find something out*, you are

    a. scared.   **b.** curious.   **c.** pounding.   **d.** crying.

3. Most likely, how does the baby dragon feel at the end of the story?

    a. sleepy   **b.** happy   **c.** mad   **d.** sad

4. What sentence best sums up the story?

    a. Dragon is afraid, so his heart pounds.

    b. Baby Dragon puts on a knight's helmet.

    c. Dragon is afraid, but he still helps.

    d. Fire comes out of Dragon's mouth.

Name: _____

Write On!

Write a story. It can be fiction or nonfiction, but part of the action must take place in a castle. Tell a fact about castles in your story.

You must also include two homophones (two words that sound the same). You can use some of the homophones in the stories, or you can think of new ones to use.

_____

_____

_____

_____

_____

_____

_____

_____

_____

_____

_____

_____

_____

_____

_____

_____

What homophones did you include?
_____ _____

Name: _____

Whizz to the Rescue!

The big wave struck! It lifted up the inflatable boat and the two little girls who were in it. It swept the boat out to sea. The girls were in danger. Their boat was very small. It was only filled with air. Who would come to their rescue? Who would come help them?

A person did not rescue the girls. They were saved by a dog! The dog's name was Whizz. Whizz was a huge dog. He was very strong. He was a good swimmer, too. Whizz had been trained to rescue people.

Whizz had been trained to swim to people who were in trouble. The people could grab on to Whizz, and Whizz would drag them to safety. Whizz saved the two little girls. Whizz saved other people, too. One time Whizz saved another dog!

1. The girls' boat was inflatable. What was it inflated with?

   a. water   b. wood   c. air   d. plastic

2. Why was Whizz able to save the girls?

   a. He did not know how to swim.

   b. He had been trained as a rescue dog.

   c. Whizz was afraid of water.

   d. Whizz liked to get in trouble.

3. When you *rescue* something, you

   a. save it or help it.

   b. drag it or drop it.

   c. grab it or sink it.

   d. save it or hurt it.

Name: _____

The Yellow Monster

Queenie said, "Is this the day? Is this the day the big, yellow monster comes? I hate that yellow monster. I don't like its enormous mouth. It's gigantic! It's so big that it can swallow Brian!"

Tex said, "Is this the day? Is this the day the big, yellow monster comes? I hate that yellow monster. I don't like its enormous mouth. It's gigantic! It's so big that it can swallow Ruby."

The big, yellow monster was coming! Queenie and Tex began to bark. They barked and barked, but it did not help. The monster kept coming. Its enormous mouth opened. It swallowed Brian! It swallowed Ruby, too!

Brian and Ruby leaned out the window. They said, "Don't worry! We will come back! This school bus will bring us home."

1. From the story, you can tell that Queenie and Tex are

   a. people.   **b.** cats.   **c.** monsters.   **d.** dogs.

2. Most likely, the story did **not** take place on

   a. Monday.   **b.** Friday.   **c.** Sunday.   **d.** Wednesday.

3. When do you find out what the monster is?

   a. at the very end of the story

   b. when you read the title

   c. at the beginning of the story

   d. in the middle of the story

Name: _____

Missing Dog

My dog is missing! Please help me find him. His name is Rocky. He is black with white paws. He has a white spot at the tip of his soft and fluffy tail.

Rocky is small, but he helps me be brave at night. He makes me feel safe and confident. When there is a storm, I hold Rocky tight. Rocky never barks or whimpers, even if there is thunder and lightning.

Rocky is six years old. I have had him since I was born. He was a gift from my Uncle Juan. Rocky stays under my pillow when I am at school.

Rocky was last seen at the pool. I had put him on a chair so that he could watch me learn how to swim. Please return Rocky if you find him! I will pay you a reward if you find my stuffed animal!

1. One of the first hints that Rocky is not a real dog is when you are told that

    a. Rocky has a soft and fluffy tail.

    b. Rocky was a gift.

    c. Rocky is small.

    d. Rocky stays under a pillow.

2. Most likely, how old is Rocky's owner?

    a. two   **b.** four   **c.** six   **d.** eight

3. Most likely, Rocky's owner

    a. feels sad.

    b. feels angry.

    c. wishes it would thunder.

    d. wants a new dog.

Name: _____

Flying Dogs

Look in the air! A helicopter is flying. It comes closer. A man drops from the air, sliding down a rope. He lands on the ground. The man is a ranger. The ranger drops, but something else drops, too. What else drops to the ground? It is a dog! Why is a dog flying in the air? Why does it drop to the ground?

A rhinoceros is a big animal. It is called a *rhino* for short. Rhinos are enormous, but they are in danger. They are being poached. What is poaching? When people hunt an animal when they shouldn't be, it is called *poaching*. Why do people poach rhinos? The people want the rhinos' horns.

The dog has been trained to work with the ranger. Together the two help protect rhinos. They ride in the helicopter. The ranger looks for poachers. When he spots a poacher, the ranger drops to the ground. The flying dog drops down, too. Together, the dog and the ranger chase after the poacher. Often, the dog catches the poacher first. The dog can smell better than the ranger. The dog can run faster, too.

1. This story is mainly about

   a. rhinos.

   b. rangers who ride in helicopters.

   c. poachers.

   d. dogs who help protect rhinos.

2. Why are rhinos being poached?

   a. People want their skin.

   b. They are enormous.

   c. People want their horns.

   d. They are good to eat.

3. Most likely, how is the dog dropped to the ground?

   a. It flies.

   b. It is lowered on a rope.

   c. It climbs down a ladder.

   d. It slides down a slide.

4. Why is paragraph 2 part of the story?

   a. to tell about the animal the dog helps protect

   b. to tell you how the dog was trained

   c. to tell you why dogs fly

   d. to tell you about people who hunt

Name: _____

Dog Crackers

The package was left at the front door. Sally saw it when she came home from school. Sally bent down and read what was written on it. The words were written in big black letters.

"Free Dog Crackers. They will really make your tail wag!"

Sally took the package into the house. She opened it up. Then she called her dog, Prince. She set a cracker on the ground in front of Prince. Prince sniffed it, but he would not eat it. "Don't be silly," Sally said to Prince. "They look fine to me. Here, I'll show you." Sally nibbled a corner of the cracker.

Then Sally felt something funny. Something behind her was wagging. Sally had grown a tail! The tail was fluffy and soft. It was about as long as Sally's arm. Over and over it waved back and forth. Sally couldn't get it to stop wagging. "I shouldn't have taken a nibble of that cracker," Sally cried.

Sally's tail wagged even faster. It wagged so fast that it knocked her over! Sally's mother came running. "Sally!" she cried. "You must have been having a wild dream. You fell out of your bed!"

1. Most likely, the author wanted you to feel _____ when you got to the end of the story.

   a. surprised   **b.** sleepy   **c.** scared   **d.** small

2. If you *nibble* something, you

   a. fall down.   **b.** take a little bite.   **c.** sniff it.   **d.** eat it all.

3. When did Sally give Prince a cracker?

   a. before she took the package into the house

   b. after she fell out of bed

   c. before she opened the package

   d. after she read the words on the package

4. What was true about Sally's tail?

   a. It was as long as her leg.   **c.** It was fluffy.

   b. It was hard.   **d.** It could not move very fast.

Name: _____

Write On!

Choose any dog but Rocky from the stories in this unit. Pretend the dog is missing. Create a "MISSING" poster that will help people find the dog and bring it back home.

MISSING

Dog's name: _____

What it looks like: _____

What it does: _____

_____

Where it was last seen: _____

Why it should be found: _____

Extra information: _____

_____

_____

Name: _____

What Fell?

The date was October 22. The year was 2012. There is a photo to prove it. What needed to be proven? What was so hard to believe? A shark fell from the sky! The shark was alive! It was two feet long!

The shark was a leopard shark. When it fell, it landed on a golf course. It fell on green grass. The shark had puncture wounds in it. The puncture wounds were like small holes. The wounds helped people know what had happened.

A big bird must have scooped up the shark. It caught it with its sharp talons. The big bird flew, carrying the shark away from the water. Then, the big bird dropped the shark. People took the shark back to the water.

1. Most likely, what made the puncture wounds in the shark?

   a. a shark in the water

   b. the bird's sharp talons

   c. the people who took the photo

   d. a golf ball

2. Why did people take a photo of the shark?

   a. They wanted to prove that sharks play golf.

   b. They didn't know that it was leopard shark.

   c. They knew that they shouldn't pick it up.

   d. They knew that the story would be hard to believe.

3. What helped people learn how the shark got there?

   a. a photo of a bird

   b. it told them

   c. its wounds

   d. someone told them

Name: _____

Lilly's Wish

Lilly looked out the window. She said, "I am tired of the rain. I am tired of the hail. I am tired of the snow. I wish something new would fall from the sky."

The next day Lilly was playing soccer with her friends. Then something hit her. It was not the ball. Lilly had been hit by a fish! Fish were dropping from the sky! Everyone on the soccer field was being hit by fish!

The fish had been scooped up into the air by a tornado. A tornado is a big wind. The fish had been carried into the air. When the wind lost its power, the fish dropped.

Fabian said, "Lilly, the next time you wish for something new to fall from the sky, wish for ice cream!"

1. What was Lilly doing when a fish hit her?

    a. swimming in a pool

    b. wishing for something new

    c. playing soccer

    d. looking at snow

2. If ice cream falls from the sky, it will be

    a. because Lilly wished for it.

    b. because a tornado scooped some up.

    c. because the fish didn't eat it.

    d. because Fabian wanted something new.

3. Most likely, how did Lilly's friends feel when the fish fell from the sky?

    a. very mad

    b. very angry

    c. very upset

    d. very surprised

Name: _____

Weather Forecast

Weather Forecast for Portland, Maine, United States of America

Date: December 21

Very cold. Cloudy. Snowstorms.

Temperature: *Low:* 0°F *High:* 10°F

A good day to make a snowman. Dress warmly!

Weather Forecast for Sydney, New South Wales, Australia

Date: December 21

Hot. Clear skies. No rain.

Temperature: *Low:* 80°F *High:* 90°F

A good day to go to the beach. Bring a sun hat!

Why are the forecasts different? Portland is a city. It is in the north. It is above the equator. Sydney is a city. It is in the south. It is below the equator. The equator is a line. It goes around the middle of Earth. It is not a real line, but it helps us know where north and south are.

Earth is tilted. It moves around the sun. This makes the seasons. The seasons are different. When it is summer in the north, it is winter in the south. When it is winter in the north, it is summer in the south!

1. Most likely, what season is it in Sydney on December 21?

    a. spring **b.** summer **c.** winter **d.** fall

2. What do we call the line we draw around the middle of Earth?

    a. the forecast

    b. the temperature

    c. the equator

    d. the season

3. Why do we draw a line around the middle of Earth?

    a. It helps us know where south and west are.

    b. It helps us know where east and west are.

    c. It helps us know where north and east are.

    d. It helps us know where north and south are.

Name: _____

Tree Rings

Scientists know when it was very cold. Scientists know when it was very hot. They know when it rained a lot. They know when it was very dry. The scientists were not there. It happened a long time ago. How do the scientists know about weather from the past?

Scientists have a special drill. Carefully, the scientists drill into a tree. They use the drill to remove a sample core from the tree. The tree is not hurt. Then, the scientists look at the core very carefully.

All trees have rings. There is one ring for each year. If a tree is 25, it will have 25 rings. The sample core has a tiny bit from each ring. The scientist counts the rings. The scientist looks closely and carefully at each ring.

What if the tree needs lots of water? In dry years, the ring will be very small. If it rains a lot, the ring will be big. What if a tree does not like lots of rain? In wet years, the ring will be small. In dry years, the ring will be big. Scientists use tree rings to tell them what the weather was like long ago!

1. If a tree is 72 years old, it will have

    a. 72 rings.   **b.** 74 rings.   **c.** 172 rings.   **d.** 174 rings.

2. If it does not rain for 10 years and a tree likes lots of water, the tree will have

    a. 10 big rings.   **c.** 10 small rings.

    b. 5 big rings and 5 small rings.   **d.** 10 big rings and 10 small rings.

3. This story is mainly about

    a. how scientists use trees to learn about past weather.

    b. how scientists drill into trees.

    c. how many rings a tree has.

    d. how scientists do not hurt trees.

4. From the story, you can tell that

    a. all trees like lots of rain.   **c.** not all trees have rings.

    b. all trees are very old.   **d.** not all trees like lots of rain.

Name: _____

The Tree

Watch out, Mr. Deer! Don't step on me! Watch out, Mrs. Bear! Don't sit on me! I want to feel the sun on my leaves. I want my roots to grow deep into the ground. I want to grow big and tall.

Hello, Fawn. I will watch you grow. You can eat the acorns that drop from my branches. Hello, Cub. I will watch you grow. You can eat the acorns that drop from my branches. Over the years, I have seen many baby deer and baby bears grow up.

I do not see fawns or bear cubs grow up anymore. Now, I see boys and girls. The boys and girls do not eat my acorns. They do not eat my acorns, but sometimes they come and have a party under my branches.

The children play at the party. They run around and around my trunk. They swing from my branches. Then, they stop to eat cake. They always put candles on the cake. The candles are lit, and then one child blows them out. I never know how many candles will be put on the cake. I wonder what the number of candles means.

1. From the story, you can tell that a baby deer is called a

   a. cub.   **b.** pup.   **c.** kitten.   **d.** fawn.

2. Most likely, the tree in the story

   a. is very weak.   **b.** is very old.   **c.** is very small.   **d.** is very sick.

3. The story is told from whose point of view?

   a. Mr. Deer

   b. a person

   c. a tree

   d. a boy or girl at a party

4. What can you tell about the tree from reading the first paragraph?

   a. It is not as tall as a deer.

   b. It is bigger than a bear.

   c. It does not have any roots.

   d. It has a big trunk.

Name: _____

Write On!

Forecast the weather! Think of a place. Pick a date. Tell what the weather will be like. Tell what you can do and what you should wear on that day.

If you forecast a tornado, what do you think will drop from the sky?

Weather forecast for _____

_____

Date: _____

Weather description: _____

_____

Temperature: *Low:* _____ *High:* _____

What to do: _____

_____

_____

_____

_____

_____

_____

_____

Name: _____

Stopping the Weed

Cattle were getting sick. Deer were getting sick. The cattle and deer were in Oregon. What was going on? The cattle and deer were eating a weed. The weed was called *tansy ragwort*. The tansy ragwort was not from Oregon. It was from far away. It was from Europe.

People wanted to stop the weed. How could they stop the weed? The people said, "Let's go to Europe. Let's see what stops the weed in Europe."

The people found a moth. They brought the moth back to Oregon. The moth laid its eggs on the tansy ragwort. Caterpillars hatched from the eggs. The caterpillars were hungry. They ate the tansy ragwort. They ate and ate and ate! They stopped the weed from growing!

1. Where did tansy ragwort grow first?

   a. Europe   **b.** Oregon   **c.** Eurasia   **d.** Oklahoma

2. Why did people in Oregon want to stop the weed?

   a. Cattle and deer did not like to eat the weed.

   b. The weed made people sick.

   c. When cattle and deer ate the weed, they got sick.

   d. They did not want the weed to grow in Europe.

3. From the story, you can tell that

   a. deer lay eggs.

   b. caterpillars lay eggs.

   c. cattle lay eggs.

   d. moths lay eggs.

Name: _____

BUZZA Food

Joey went to the store to buy cat food. The lady in the store said, "Feed your cat BEST food. Do not feed the cat BUZZA food. BUZZA food is for cats from a place far away."

Joey fed his cat BEST food. Soon he needed more food. Joey went to the store. Joey said, "The lady is not here. I am going to buy BUZZA food so I can see what happens."

Joey brought the BUZZA food home. He opened the bag and poured some of it into a bowl. When Joey's cat ate it, his cat started to make a funny sound! It started to buzz and buzz! Joey's cat was unhappy. It couldn't purr. It could only buzz. Joey said, "No more BUZZA food for you!"

1. Who should buy BUZZA food?

   a. no one who has a cat

   b. everyone who has a cat

   c. no one who has a cat from a place far away

   d. someone who has a cat from a place far away

2. Why was Joey's cat unhappy?

   a. It was hungry.

   b. It couldn't purr.

   c. It wanted to keep buzzing.

   d. It wanted Joey to buy more BUZZA food.

3. When you *need* something,

   a. you open it.

   b. you pour it.

   c. you must have it.

   d. you see what happens.

Name: _____

Rose's Diary

July 18, 2010

I got my wish! I wanted a snake for my birthday. I got a boa. It is small. It is one foot long.

July 18, 2015

My snake is not a good pet any longer. It is too big. It is ten feet long! It costs too much to feed it. I am going to set it free in the Florida Everglades.

July 18, 2020

All the native animals in the Florida Everglades are being eaten. They are being eaten by big boas. The boas are not native. They came from other countries. People let the boas go in the Everglades when they were tired of taking care of them. I am sorry now that I set my snake free in the Everglades.

Park rangers are trying to keep the native animals safe. They trap the boas. They take them away. One boa was 20 feet long! It weighed 250 pounds! When I grow up, I will be a park ranger. I will help native animals stay safe.

1. Boas are not native to the Everglades because

    a. they are so big.

    b. they weigh so much.

    c. they came from other countries.

    d. they cost a lot to feed.

2. At the end of the story, how did Rose feel about setting her snake free in the Everglades?

    a. glad   **b.** mad   **c.** happy   **d.** sorry

3. Most likely, the Florida Everglades is

    a. a big park.   **c.** a swimming pool.

    b. a small city.   **d.** a school.

Name: _____

The Vine That Ate

The vine was taking over! It was growing everywhere. It was growing on fences. It was growing on poles. It was growing on walls. It was covering the hills. It was growing over grass and trees. The vine was called *kudzu*.

Kudzu did not come from the United States. Kudzu came from Japan. It was brought to the United States from Japan. Farmers in the south were told, "Grow kudzu. It will help stop soil from being washed away." The farmers did what they were told. They planted kudzu. They wanted to keep good dirt from washing away.

At first, everyone liked the kudzu. It grew fast. It was pretty. The problem was that it didn't stop growing. It grew and grew and grew! People began to call kudzu "the vine that ate the south."

All kinds of things were tried to stop the vine. The vine just kept growing. Then, one city hired a man who had a lot of workers. The workers were goats! The goats ate and ate and ate. They helped the people stop the kudzu from taking over the city!

1. Why did the farmers plant the kudzu?

    a. They wanted goats to have something to eat.

    b. They wanted to be like Japan.

    c. They wanted something to cover the hills.

    d. They wanted to stop their soil from washing away.

2. How did everyone feel about kudzu at first?

    a. They liked it.   **c.** They didn't like it.

    b. They called it "the vine that ate   **d.** They didn't think it was pretty.
       the south."

3. Another word for *dirt* is

    a. goat.   **b.** soil.   **c.** vine.   **d.** pole.

4. This story is mainly about

    a. a new plant to the United States.   **c.** all the vines in Japan.

    b. the life of goats.   **d.** cities in the south of Japan.

Name: _____

King Midas

King Midas loved gold. He loved gold more than anything in the world. King Midas always wanted more gold. "There is never enough gold," he said. "Everything should be gold."

One day, King Midas saw a strange little man. The little man was wearing a green coat and tall black boots. The little man said, "King Midas, I will grant you a wish. What do you wish for?"

King Midas said, "I wish for gold, of course! I want everything I touch to turn to gold." That sounds like a good wish, but is it?

King Midas tried to drink. His drink turned to gold! King Midas got very thirsty because he could not drink anything. King Midas tried to eat. His food turned to gold! King Midas got very hungry because he could not eat anything. King Midas tried to hug his daughter. His daughter turned to gold! She was cold and stiff. She could not move or talk. King Midas started to cry. He was very sad that his daughter could not move or talk.

The strange little man in the green coat and tall black boots came back. "I will give you another wish," he said. Do you know what King Midas wished for?

1. Most likely, King Midas's new wish was
   a. that his daughter would stay stiff and cold.
   b. that everything he touched would no longer be gold.
   c. that only his food and drink would not be gold.
   d. that everything he touched would still turn to gold.

2. Why did King Midas get thirsty?
   a. He was thirsty from running around the castle.
   b. The strange man did not give him a drink.
   c. He gave his drink to his daughter.
   d. Everything he tried to drink turned to gold.

3. From the story, you can tell that
   a. gold is better than anything in the world.
   b. King Midas wanted his daughter to be made of gold.
   c. gold is not always the best thing in the world.
   d. King Midas made a good wish at the beginning of the story.

4. How many wishes was King Midas given?
   a. one   b. two   c. three   d. four

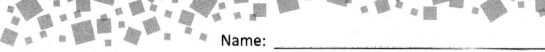

Name: _____

Write On!

Pick any of the stories from this unit except the story "Rose's Diary." Then imagine that you are the person in the story or someone with the same problem. Write three diary entries that fit with the story you chose.

Date: _____

What I want: _____

Date: _____

Problem with what I got: _____

Date: _____

How I fixed the problem: _____

Name: _____

Muscles

Say the word "muscle." Did you think strong or weak? Most people think "strong." Did you think big or small? Most people think "big." A person with muscles can run fast. They can swim far. They can lift heavy things.

Say the word "muscle." Did you think of a mouse? Most people do not. They do not think a mouse is strong. They do not think a mouse is big. They think a mouse is small. They think it is weak.

Long ago, people spoke Latin. Our word "muscle" comes from Latin. It comes from the Latin word "musculus." What does musculus mean in Latin? It means little mouse! What did people long ago think our muscles looked like? They thought our muscles looked like little mice running under our skins!

1. The word *muscle* comes from

    a. a new word.

    b. a strong mouse.

    c. a Latin word.

    d. a weak mouse.

2. From the story, you can tell that

    a. words change over time.

    b. words never change.

    c. there are never new words.

    d. there were no words long ago.

3. Think about the words **big** and **small**. How are they different? What words are different in the same way?

    a. mouse and mice

    b. tall and high

    c. speak and talk

    d. strong and weak

Name: _____

What Mia Wanted

Mia lived on a farm. She was usually very happy. One day, she would not stop crying. Over and over, she said that she wanted pancakes. Jack told Mia that she could have pancakes. He would cook pancakes. They could eat pancakes for lunch.

Jack thought Mia would be happy. She wasn't! She cried. She screamed. Over and over, she said, "Don't cook pancakes! Don't cook pancakes! I don't want pancakes for lunch!"

Jack told Mia he would not cook pancakes. Then he asked her what she wanted for lunch. Mia cried, "Pancakes!" Then Mia picked up a chicken. Mia said, "This is my chicken, Pancakes. I named him Pancakes because of his color. His feathers are the color of pancakes! I don't want you to cook Pancakes for lunch. I want a sandwich for lunch."

1. From the story, you can tell that Jack
   a. knew that Mia wanted a sandwich for lunch.
   b. did not want Mia to stop crying.
   c. knew that Mia had a chicken named "Pancakes."
   d. did not know that Mia had a chicken named "Pancakes."

2. What did Mia think Jack was saying?
   a. He would not make lunch.
   b. He would cook her chicken.
   c. He wanted Mia to cry.
   d. He wanted Mia to scream.

3. Why did Mia name her chicken "Pancakes"?
   a. She liked to eat pancakes.
   b. It was the same color as pancakes.
   c. She always knew where her chicken was.
   d. It was round like a pancake.

Name: _____

Ahoy or Hello?

The phone rings. You answer it. What do you say? You say "hello." Why do we say hello? To know, you must go back in time. Go back to 1876. That is the year that the first phone was made.

The phone was new. People did not know how to answer it. What was best? Was it best to ask, "What do you want?" Was it best to ask, "Who is talking?" A man named Bell helped make the first phone. Bell liked the word "ahoy." Why did Bell think that people should say "ahoy" when they answered the phone?

A ship meets another ship. A sailor meets another sailor. What do they say? The sailors greet each other by saying, "Ahoy!" Bell said, "We should greet each other on the phone the same way. We should say, 'Ahoy!'"

A man named Edison said no. He said he had a better way. He wanted people to say "Hello." Before then, hello was not a word! By 1880, everyone said hello when they answered the phone. Today, we say hello even when we are not answering the phone. We say it at school. We say it at home. We say it whenever we greet people.

1. How did Bell think we should answer the phone?

   a. by asking, "What do you want?"

   b. by saying, "Ahoy!"

   c. by asking, "Who is talking?"

   d. by saying, "Hello."

2. When you say *hello* to someone, you are

   a. greeting them.   c. making a new thing.

   b. meeting a ship.   d. going back in time.

3. Why didn't people know how to answer the phone in 1876?

   a. No one went to school.

   b. The phone was old.

   c. No one talked.

   d. The phone was new.

Name: _____

Jumbo

You want popcorn. You don't want a little. You want a lot. You do not ask for the small bag. You do not ask for the medium bag. You want the biggest bag. You want the largest bag. You ask for the jumbo-sized bag.

In English, jumbo means big. It means large. It means huge. When did the word "jumbo" start meaning "something huge"? Long ago, "jumbo" did not mean big. It didn't mean large. It wasn't an English word!

In 1860, an elephant was sent to a zoo. The zookeepers named the elephant. They named him "Jumbo." Jumbo was huge! He was the biggest elephant people had ever seen. People came from all over to see Jumbo. He became famous. People talked about him. People wrote about him. If someone called something jumbo, people knew what they meant. They meant it was big. It was huge. Today jumbo is a word. It means big. It means huge.

An elephant helped make a new word!

1. Another title for this story might be

    a. "A New Word."

    b. "Elephants."

    c. "Popcorn."

    d. "Animals in the Zoo."

2. When something is *famous*, it is

    a. angry.   **b.** an animal.   **c.** large.   **d.** well known.

3. What can you tell about elephants from reading the story?

    a. They are all big.

    b. They are all small.

    c. They are not all the same size.

    d. They are all in zoos.

4. When was Jumbo sent to the zoo?

    a. 1760   **b.** 1860   **c.** 1960   **d.** 2060

Name: _____

What Henry Wanted

Henry didn't like the dark. When it was time to sleep, Henry kept a small light on. He said, "The light helps me sleep." It was time to go to sleep. Henry's babysitter made sure a small light was on. Did Henry go to sleep? No, he didn't! What did Henry do? He said, "I want Night! I want Night to come! I won't go to sleep until Night is here!"

The babysitter turned off the light. She said, "It is night and dark. Now go to sleep." Did Henry go to sleep? No, he didn't! What did Henry do? He started yelling! He said, "Turn on the light! I want my small light! I do not want it to be dark, but I want Night."

The babysitter told Henry to stop yelling. She said, "If I turn on the light, the night is not dark. Do you want the light or not?"

Then, something came into Henry's room. Henry smiled a big smile. He said, "Oh, Night, there you are. It's time to sleep." Then, the babysitter understood. Night was a cat! Both Henry and Night fell asleep. All through the night, Night purred, and the little light kept the dark away.

1. Why didn't the babysitter understand what Henry wanted?

    a. She didn't know it was dark at night.

    b. Henry didn't tell her what he wanted.

    c. She didn't know Night was the name of Henry's cat.

    d. Henry didn't stop yelling.

2. Look back in the story. When "night" starts with a capital N,

    a. it means Henry's cat.   c. it means it is time to go to sleep.

    b. it means it is dark.   d. it means Henry is sleeping.

3. This story is mainly about

    a. a small light.   c. what Henry's babysitter did.

    b. cats.   d. what Henry needed to go to sleep.

4. How many things helped Henry go to sleep?

    a. one   b. two   c. three   d. four

Name: _____

Write On!

You are talking to a friend on the phone. Write down your name and your friend's name. Answer the phone by saying "Ahoy" or "Hello."

Tell your friend about one of the stories you read. Imagine what he or she might say to you.

_____ : _____
Your name

_____

_____ : _____
Friend's name

_____

_____ : _____
Your name

_____

_____ : _____
Friend's name

_____

_____ : _____
Your name

_____

_____ : _____
Friend's name

_____

Name: _____

Teeth and More Teeth

Think about your mouth. Think about how big it is. How many teeth do you have? Most children your age have 20 baby teeth. Your baby teeth will fall out. Then, 32 more teeth will grow in.

Now, think about a pin. Think about the head of a pin. It is very small. One animal has a mouth this small! Like you, this animal has teeth. How many teeth does this animal have? It does not have less. It does not have the same. It has more! It has a lot more! It can have thousands more! What animal could this be? It is a snail. Snails can have 25,000 teeth!

Think about where your teeth are. Your teeth have roots. The roots keep your teeth from falling out. Your roots grow into your jaw. Snails are different. Their teeth are not rooted to their jaws. Where are their teeth? All their teeth are on their tongues!

1. From the story, you can tell that your teeth

   a. are a lot smaller than a snail's teeth.

   b. are about the same size as a snail's teeth.

   c. are a lot bigger than a snail's teeth.

   d. are in the same place as a snail's teeth.

2. Your teeth have roots that grow

   a. on your tongue.

   b. into your jaw.

   c. in the ground.

   d. on a snail.

3. A new title for this story might be

   a. "Your Teeth and Snail Teeth."

   b. "Baby Teeth."

   c. "How Many Teeth Will You Grow?"

   d. "All About the Animal with the Biggest Teeth."

Name: _____

The Missing Tooth

Kate's tooth was loose. Kate put her finger on her tooth. She wiggled it back and forth. She could feel it move. Kate wiggled and wiggled her tooth some more. No matter how many times and how hard Kate wiggled it, the tooth would not come out.

Kate was the only one in her class who had not lost a tooth. Some boys and girls had lost four! Their big teeth had already grown in!

Kate's teacher handed out apple slices. She said, "We are going to taste red, yellow, and green apples. We will vote. We will see what color apple people like the best."

Kate took a bite of red. Then, she wiggled her tooth. She took a bite of yellow. Then, she wiggled her tooth some more. She took a bite of green. She went to wiggle her tooth, but she couldn't! Kate's tooth was missing! Where was the missing tooth? It was stuck in the rest of Kate's apple slice!

1. Think about the words **tooth** and **teeth**. Think about how they are alike. What words are alike in the same way?

    a. foot and toes

    b. foot and socks

    c. foot and legs

    d. foot and feet

2. What color apple slice was Kate's tooth in?

    a. yellow   **b.** green   **c.** red   **d.** pink

3. Most likely, how did Kate feel at the end of the story?

    a. mad because she could not find her tooth

    b. sad because she lost her tooth

    c. happy because she found her tooth

    d. glad because she liked red apples

Name: _____

Wild Animal Dentist

A dentist got a phone call. This dentist did not work on people. He worked on animals. He would go to zoos. He would go to parks. He would go where big wild animals needed him.

A jaguar had been found. The jaguar was in Belize. It had been found in the jungle. The jaguar had a broken leg. It also had a mouth of broken and bloody teeth. It could not hunt. It needed help.

People in Belize could fix the big cat's leg. They could not fix its teeth. They called the dentist and asked for help. The dentist got on a plane. He flew to Belize. He went into the jungle. He went to where the jaguar had been found.

There was no electricity. There were no x-ray machines. The dentist did the best he could. He put the jaguar to sleep. He started fixing its teeth. The dentist was only halfway done when the jaguar put his head up! The jaguar was waking up! The dentist acted fast! Quickly, he gave something to the jaguar. He gave it something to make it fall asleep again!

1. From the story, you can tell that a jaguar

    a. is a tame animal.

    b. is a big cat.

    c. lives in the sea.

    d. lives on a farm.

2. How did the dentist get to Belize?

    a. He went on a boat.

    b. He flew on a plane.

    c. He walked very quickly.

    d. He drove in a car.

3. The best title for this story is

    a. "All About Jaguars."

    b. "All About Dentists."

    c. "The Dentist and the Jaguar."

    d. "The Jaguar with the Broken Leg."

Name: _____

One a Day

When you are born, you have no teeth. One animal is different. When this animal is born, it has a full set of teeth. It does not need soft baby food. It can bite and chew immediately.

You will lose 20 baby teeth. You will have spaces in your mouth until the new teeth grow in. One animal sheds its teeth all the time. It may shed thousands and thousands of teeth over its lifetime! This animal will not have problems with spaces in its mouth. It does not take a long time for a missing tooth to be replaced. A new tooth will move into place in just one day!

What animal is born with a full set of teeth? What animal can shed thousands of teeth? What animal can replace a lost tooth in just one day? It is a shark.

You have one row of teeth in each jaw. Most sharks have 15 rows of teeth. Some sharks have 50 rows of teeth! What shape are the teeth? The shape is not always the same. It depends on what the shark eats.

1. From the story, you can tell that if you *shed* something, you

   a. lose it.   **b.** replace it.   **c.** grow it.   **d.** chew it.

2. Why doesn't a baby shark need its mother to help it find soft food?

   a. It has spaces in its mouth.

   b. It can lose thousands of teeth.

   c. The shape of the tooth is not always the same.

   d. It is born with a full set of teeth.

3. This story is mainly about

   a. what sharks eat.   **c.** different kinds of sharks.

   b. shark teeth.   **d.** replacing animal teeth.

4. A person says, "This kind of shark eats seals." Most likely, the person

   a. saw how many rows of teeth the shark had.

   b. knew that the shark would shed thousands of teeth.

   c. saw the shape of the shark's tooth.

   d. knew that sharks could replace a tooth in a day.

Name: _____

Horse Talk

Prescott said, "Jackson, we are the two best-looking horses. We are both big. We are both strong. I like the man who rides us. I like that he takes turns riding us. I like it when we ride in parades. I like that he takes such good care of us. We must be his favorite horses."

Jackson said, "I like that our hair gets brushed daily. I like that we get blankets when it is cold. I like that we get new straw bedding every night. I like that our hooves are polished every morning. I do not like that our teeth are brushed daily. Why are our teeth brushed every day?"

Prescott said, "The man who rides us is George Washington. He is the president. He doesn't have any teeth. They were rotten, so they all had to be pulled out. Now, he has fake teeth. The fake teeth hurt his mouth. They are painful to wear."

Jackson said, "Oh, now I know why he has our teeth brushed every day. He doesn't want us to lose our teeth. There is no such thing as fake teeth for horses!"

1. This story has many facts. What cannot be true?
   a. George Washington had horses named Prescott and Jackson.
   b. George Washington's horses knew George had fake teeth.
   c. George Washington had fake teeth.
   d. George Washington had his horse's teeth brushed.

2. What happened first?
   a. George Washington got fake teeth.
   b. George Washington had his teeth pulled.
   c. George Washington's teeth were rotten.
   d. George Washington's fake teeth were painful.

3. Most likely, George Washington's favorite horses are
   a. lazy.   b. spotted.   c. brown.   d. strong.

4. George Washington rides Prescott on Monday. Most likely, he will
   a. ride Jackson on Tuesday.   c. never ride Jackson.
   b. ride Jackson on Wednesday.   d. ride Prescott on Thursday.

Name: _____

Write On!

How are your teeth different from a shark's? Use the information from "One a Day" to help you answer the question.

_____

_____

_____

_____

_____

_____

_____

_____

_____

_____

_____

_____

_____

_____

_____

_____

_____

_____

Name: _____

Carried by a Yak

A climber wants to climb the world's highest mountain. The climber wants to climb Mount Everest. It will take many days. The climber will need lots of food. The climber will need a tent and other supplies. Who helps the climber get the food and supplies to the mountain? A yak does!

A yak has horns. The horns are long and curved. When it snows, the yak uses its horns. It scrapes up snow and finds grass to eat under the snow. A yak has thick, shaggy fur. The thick, shaggy fur keeps the yak very warm. What happens to the yak if it goes in ice-cold water? The yak stays warm! The yak's thick, shaggy fur keeps it warm!

1. From the story, you can tell that

    a. yaks live in the water.

    b. yaks cannot carry things.

    c. yaks can climb higher than people.

    d. yaks live where it is cold and snowy.

2. What does a yak use its horns for?

    a. to scrape up snow

    b. to stay warm

    c. to help it swim

    d. to brush its thick, shaggy fur

3. Why might climbers use yaks to help bring supplies to Mount Everest?

    a. There are lots of stores on Mount Everest.

    b. Climbers want to teach yaks how to climb.

    c. There are not any good roads for cars and trucks.

    d. Climbers don't need many supplies.

Name: _____

Molly the Yak

Molly said, "I am a yak. I am the best kind of mammal in the world. No other mammal lives as high as I do. I have really big lungs. My lungs are much larger than those of the cattle that live on the low lands. My large lungs help me live up high. Up high, the air is thin. There is less oxygen. With my large lungs, I can take in more air. I can get more oxygen.

"I help climbers get supplies to Mount Everest. One time, a box on my back broke open. Long, round cans fell out. Each can weighed about six pounds. I asked another yak what was in the cans. He told me that they were oxygen tanks. Many climbers need extra oxygen when they climb Mount Everest because the air is so thin. I bet that those climbers wish they had lungs as big as mine!"

1. What is one way yaks are different than cattle?

   a. Yaks live on the low lands.

   b. Yaks live on land.

   c. Yaks have larger lungs.

   d. Yaks are mammals.

2. From the story, you can tell that air is partly made up of

   a. cheese.   b. apples.   c. cake.   d. oxygen.

3. What answer sums up the story best?

   a. A yak talks with another yak.

   b. A yak climbs Mount Everest.

   c. A yak sees oxygen tanks.

   d. A yak talks about her lungs.

Name: _____

A Choice of Ropes

Brad and Jeff had to make a choice. There were two sets of fixed ropes. One set went across rocks. The other set was buried under two feet of snow. The buried set was across a snow slope. It would have been easier for Brad and Jeff to use the unburied ropes. It would have been faster.

Brad and Jeff did not take the easy way. They took the hard way. It took two hours to clear the ropes of snow. It was hard because Brad and Jeff were up high. There was little air. The lack of air made them get tired quickly.

Why did Brad and Jeff take the hard way? They did it for Eric. Eric was on their team. Eric could not see. He was blind. For Eric, it would be easier to go up the snow slope. There would be no rocks to trip over. Everyone said that a blind person could not climb Mount Everest. They were wrong. Eric showed that, with help, people can do anything.

1. What did Brad and Jeff decide to do?

   a. Use the set of ropes across the rocks.

   b. Take the fast choice.

   c. Use the set of buried ropes.

   d. Take the easy choice.

2. Why did Brad and Jeff make this choice?

   a. They wanted to work hard.

   b. They wanted to help someone on their team.

   c. They didn't want to trip over rocks.

   d. They knew that they would get tired quickly.

3. When do you find out why Brad and Jeff made the choice that they did?

   a. when you read the title

   b. when you read the first paragraph

   c. when you read the second paragraph

   d. when you read the third paragraph

Name: _____

Eggs on the Mountain

Mount Everest is a big mountain. It is very tall. It is the tallest mountain in the world. What if you hiked to the top of Mount Everest? Could you boil an egg? Could you boil it until it is cooked? Could you make the egg hard?

Once water boils, it will not get hotter. Boil, boil, and boil some more, but the temperature will not go up.

Down low, boiling water is very hot. It is hot enough to make an egg hard. Up high, it is not the same.

Up high, water boils at a lower temperature. This is because there is less air. It is easier for water to boil when less air is pressing down on it.

The yellow part of the egg is the yolk. The yolk will cook on Mount Everest. The boiling water is warm enough. The white part of the egg will not cook. It will not get hard. The boiling water will not be hot enough.

1. From the story, you can tell that the temperature of boiling water

    a. never changes.

    b. is lower when you are on top of Mount Everest.

    c. is never hot enough to cook an egg white.

    d. is always hot enough to cook an egg white.

2. Water in a pot starts to boil. What temperature is the water after it boils for ten minutes?

    a. warmer than when it started boiling

    b. colder than when it started boiling

    c. the same as when it started boiling

    d. 300 degrees

3. What part of the egg will cook in boiling water on Mount Everest?

    a. the white   **b.** the yolk   **c.** all of it   **d.** none of it

4. Most likely, people have trouble breathing on the top of Mount Everest because

    a. there is less air.   **c.** there is more air.

    b. the air is warm.   **d.** the air is boiling.

Name: _____

Sherpa Guide

My name is Tenzing. I was named after a great Sherpa guide. The Sherpas live near the highest mountain in the world. They live near Mount Everest. Sherpas help climbers. Climbers come from all over the world. They all want to climb Mount Everest. Sherpas help them.

Sherpas carry food. They carry tents. They carry ropes. Sherpas set up camp. They make bridges. What do they use to make the bridges? They use ladders. The bridges are not over water. They are over deep holes in the ice. The Sherpas fix ropes, too. When they fix the rope, they bolt it to the rock. Climbers can hold on to the ropes. The ropes help keep them safe.

Years ago, no one could climb Mount Everest. Climbers tried and tried. Then two people did it. One of them was Tenzing. The other one was a man named Hillary. Tenzing and Hillary were the first to reach the top. They stood where no one had ever stood before. I am a Sherpa. One day, I will follow in Tenzing's footsteps. Just like Tenzing, I will stand on top of the world.

1. A *guide* is

    a. a person who shows someone the way.

    b. a kind of bridge.

    c. a person who is always first.

    d. a hole in the ice.

2. What does the writer mean when he says that he will "stand on the top of the world"?

    a. He will get to the top of Mount Everest.

    b. He will build a bridge.

    c. He will set up camp and hold on to a rope.

    d. He will cross a ladder.

3. This story is mainly about

    a. tall mountains.

    b. following footsteps.

    c. climbers from all over the world.

    d. a Sherpa guide and who he is named after.

4. When a rope is *fixed*, it is

    a. used for jumping.

    b. bolted to a rock.

    c. over a deep hole in the ice.

    d. tied to a ladder.

Name: _____

Write On!

Imagine that you are climbing the highest mountain in the world!

- Tell what mountain you are climbing.
- Tell what helped you get your supplies to the mountain.
- Tell who is helping to guide you.
- Tell why you might feel tired.
- Tell if you make it to the top!
- Tell if anything scary happens.

_____

_____

_____

_____

_____

_____

_____

_____

_____

_____

_____

_____

_____

_____

_____

Tracking Sheet

Unit 1 (pages 6–11)		Unit 7 (pages 42–47)		Unit 13 (pages 78–83)	
A Slow Animal		Where in the World?		What Fell?	
What Animal Am I?		A Place to Love		Lilly's Wish	
When a Sloth Is Cold		Letter to Grandpa		Weather Forecast	
Green Hair		Down Under		Tree Rings	
The Oddest Thing		The Silly Bridge		The Tree	
Write On!		Write On!		Write On!	
Unit 2 (pages 12–17)		**Unit 8 (pages 48–53)**		**Unit 14 (pages 84–89)**	
The Coldest		Mary's Lamb		Stopping the Weed	
Danger on the Ice!		Little Piggy		BUZZA Food	
A Penguin Play		Jack and Jill		Rose's Diary	
A Fight		Where Was Tom?		The Vine That Ate	
Pete's Wish		Hickory, Dickory, Dock		King Midas	
Write On!		Write On!		Write On!	
Unit 3 (pages 18–23)		**Unit 9 (pages 54–59)**		**Unit 15 (pages 90–95)**	
Six Times		Hungry Ants		Muscles	
Why the Moon Gets Big and Small		Little and Big		What Mia Wanted	
New Life Form Report		Book Report		Ahoy or Hello?	
Taller, Taller, Shorter		Not a Spider		Jumbo	
Strange Salt, Strange Pepper		Grasshopper and Ant		What Henry Wanted	
Write On!		Write On!		Write On!	
Unit 4 (pages 24–29)		**Unit 10 (pages 60–65)**		**Unit 16 (pages 96–101)**	
Suitcase Surprise		A Kind of Boat		Teeth and More Teeth	
Rules, Rules, Rules		Birthday Treat		The Missing Tooth	
The Bone Proof		Captain's Log		Wild Animal Dentist	
Apple Picking		Kayaks		One a Day	
Writing Dots		The Largest Animal		Horse Talk	
Write On!		Write On!		Write On!	
Unit 5 (pages 30–35)		**Unit 11 (pages 66–71)**		**Unit 17 (pages 102–107)**	
What Am I?		Castle Stairs		Carried by a Yak	
Sad People		The King's Sword		Molly the Yak	
Clues		A Note to My Reader		A Choice of Ropes	
What Reptile?		Castle Windows		Eggs on the Mountain	
Not Strange		The Scary Sound		Sherpa Guide	
Write On!		Write On!		Write On!	
Unit 6 (pages 36–41)		**Unit 12 (pages 72–77)**			
Fairy Tale		Whizz to the Rescue!			
Silly and Smarty		The Yellow Monster			
A Special Kind of Joke		Missing Dog			
The Princess and the Pea		Flying Dogs			
The Other Princess		Dog Crackers			
Write On!		Write On!			

Answer Key

Answer Key

Unit 1

A Slow Animal (page 6)

1. c   2. b   3. a

What Animal Am I? (page 7)

1. d   2. d   3. b

When a Sloth Is Cold (page 8)

1. c   2. a   3. d

Green Hair (page 9)

1. b   2. a   3. c

The Oddest Thing (page 10)

1. d   2. a   3. c   4. b

Unit 2

The Coldest (page 12)

1. d   2. d   3. b

Danger on the Ice! (page 13)

1. a   2. a   3. d

A Penguin Play (page 14)

1. d   2. b   3. a

A Fight (page 15)

1. b   2. a   3. c   4. a

Pete's Wish (page 16)

1. c   2. c   3. b

4. back is black, front is white

Unit 3

Six Times (page 18)

1. d   2. b   3. c

Why the Moon Gets Big and Small (page 19)

1. a   2. c   3. a

New Life Form Report (page 20)

1. b   2. d   3. a

Taller, Taller, Shorter (page 21)

1. a   2. d   3. c   4. b

Strange Salt, Strange Pepper (page 22)

1. d   2. c   3. a   4. b

Unit 4

Suitcase Surprise (page 24)

1. d   2. b   3. a

Rules, Rules, Rules (page 25)

1. c   2. d   3. a

The Bone Proof (page 26)

1. b   2. b   3. d

Apple Picking (page 27)

1. d   2. b   3. a   4. c

Writing Dots (page 28)

1. a   2. d   3. d   4. c

Unit 5

What Am I? (page 30)

1. a   2. d   3. b

Sad People (page 31)

1. d   2. c   3. b

Clues (page 32)

1. c   2. a   3. c

What Reptile? (page 33)

1. b   2. c   3. d   4. b

Not Strange (page 34)

1. a   2. c   3. d   4. b

Unit 6

Fairy Tale (page 36)

1. c   2. b   3. a

Silly and Smarty (page 37)

1. b   2. d   3. c

A Special Kind of Joke (page 38)

1. d   2. a   3. c

The Princess and the Pea (page 39)

1. c   2. d   3. a   4. b

The Other Princess (page 40)

1. a   2. c   3. d   4. b

Answer Key *(cont.)*

Unit 7

Where in the World? (page 42)

1. a   2. d   3. c

A Place to Love (page 43)

1. b   2. c   3. d

Letter to Grandpa (page 44)

1. c   2. b   3. a

Down Under (page 45)

1. a   2. c   3. b   4. a

The Silly Bridge (page 46)

1. c   2. a   3. d   4. b

Unit 8

Mary's Lamb (page 48)

1. b   2. a   3. a

Little Piggy (page 49)

1. c   2. b   3. a

Jack and Jill (page 50)

1. d   2. b   3. a

Where Was Tom? (page 51)

1. d   2. b   3. c   4. d

Hickory, Dickory, Dock (page 52)

1. a   2. d   3. a   4. c

Unit 9

Hungry Ants (page 54)

1. d   2. b   3. a

Little and Big (page 55)

1. c   2. a   3. d

Book Report (page 56)

1. a   2. b   3. d

Not a Spider (page 57)

1. b   2. c   3. d   4. a

Grasshopper and Ant (page 58)

1. c   2. c   3. b   4. a

Unit 10

A Kind of Boat (page 60)

1. a   2. d   3. c

Birthday Treat (page 61)

1. b   2. a   3. c

Captain's Log (page 62)

1. b   2. d   3. a

Kayaks (page 63)

1. d   2. c   3. a   4. b

The Largest Animal (page 64)

1. d   2. a   3. c   4. b

Unit 11

Castle Stairs (page 66)

1. c   2. d   3. a

The King's Sword (page 67)

1. b   2. c   3. a

A Note to My Reader (page 68)

1. b   2. c   3. a   4. b

Castle Windows (page 69)

1. a   2. d   3. a   4. d

The Scary Sound (page 70)

1. d   2. b   3. b   4. c

Unit 12

Whizz to the Rescue! (page 72)

1. c   2. b   3. a

The Yellow Monster (page 73)

1. d   2. c   3. a

Missing Dog (page 74)

1. d   2. c   3. a

Flying Dogs (page 75)

1. d   2. c   3. b   4. a

Dog Crackers (page 76)

1. a   2. b   3. d   4. c

Answer Key *(cont.)*

Unit 13

What Fell? (page 78)

1. b   2. d   3. c

Lilly's Wish (page 79)

1. c   2. b   3. d

Weather Forecast (page 80)

1. b   2. c   3. d

Tree Rings (page 81)

1. a   2. c   3. a   4. d

The Tree (page 82)

1. d   2. b   3. c   4. a

Unit 14

Stopping the Weed (page 84)

1. a   2. c   3. d

BUZZA Food (page 85)

1. d   2. b   3. c

Rose's Diary (page 86)

1. c   2. d   3. a

The Vine That Ate (page 87)

1. d   2. a   3. b   4. a

King Midas (page 88)

1. b   2. d   3. c   4. b

Unit 15

Muscles (page 90)

1. c   2. a   3. d

What Mia Wanted (page 91)

1. d   2. b   3. b

Ahoy or Hello? (page 92)

1. b   2. a   3. d

Jumbo (page 93)

1. a   2. d   3. c   4. b

What Henry Wanted (page 94)

1. c   2. a   3. d   4. b

Unit 16

Teeth and More Teeth (page 96)

1. c   2. b   3. a

The Missing Tooth (page 97)

1. d   2. b   3. c

Wild Animal Dentist (page 98)

1. b   2. b   3. c

One a Day (page 99)

1. a   2. d   3. b   4. c

Horse Talk (page 100)

1. b   2. c   3. d   4. a

Unit 17

Carried by a Yak (page 102)

1. d   2. a   3. c

Molly the Yak (page 103)

1. c   2. d   3. d

A Choice of Ropes (page 104)

1. c   2. b   3. d

Eggs on the Mountain (page 105)

1. b   2. c   3. b   4. a

Sherpa Guide (page 106)

1. a   2. a   3. d   4. b